Why Teach?

Why Teach?

Notes and Questions from a Life in Education

James Nehring

ROWMAN & LITTLEFIELD
Lanham • Boulder • New York • London

Published by Rowman & Littlefield
A wholly owned subsidiary of The Rowman & Littlefield Publishing Group, Inc.
4501 Forbes Boulevard, Suite 200, Lanham, Maryland 20706
www.rowman.com

Unit A, Whitacre Mews, 26-34 Stannary Street, London SE11 4AB

British Library Cataloguing in Publication Information Available

Library of Congress Cataloging-in-Publication Data

Nehring, James, author.
Why teach? : notes and questions from a life in education / James Nehring.
pages cm
Includes bibliographical references.
ISBN 978-1-4758-2035-5 (cloth : alk. paper) -- ISBN 978-1-4758-2036-2 (pbk. : alk. paper) -- ISBN
978-1-4758-2037-9 (electronic)
1. Nehring, James. 2. Teachers--United States--Biography. 3. Teaching--United States. 4. Education,
Humanistic. I. Title.
LA2317.N44A3 2015
371.10092--dc23
2015017135

Printed in the United States of America

For Ken

Contents

Foreword   xiii

Acknowledgments   xv

Introduction   xvii

    Indoor Work   xvii

    How This Book Came to Be   xviii

    The Heart of It All   xix

I: Entry   **1**

   1   3

    Ditch of Distinction   3

    Time to Move On   4

    Holding Kids Hostage   7

    Chapter 1: Reflection Questions   7

    Suggested Reading   8

   2   9

    Teaching and Telling   9

    Student Will Be Able To . . .   12

    Real Students   13

    Day One   15

    In Search of a First Job   16

    Chapter 2: Reflection Questions   16

    Suggested Reading   17

II: Beginner   **19**

   3   21

    What Are Kids Like?   21

    That One Student   21

    Losing My Way   24

    Finding My Way Back   26

    Choosing Who to Become   28

    Chapter 3: Reflection Questions   31

    Suggested Reading   31

   4   33

    Teaching and Coaching   33

    Two Boys   35

Three Girls   36
Teaching Gandhi   38
New Jeopardy   40
Chapter 4: Reflection Questions   42
Suggested Reading   42

5   45
A Pleasant Routine   45
How Do You Ask a Question?   45
A Life Raft Appears   50
Pretty Much It   51
Chapter 5: Reflection Questions   53
Suggested Reading   54

6   55
Mystery and Results   55
Pitching Stories   56
Unmapped Territory   59
Chapter 6: Reflection Questions   60
Suggested Reading   61

III: Resist   63
7   65
Uppity Teacher   65
Photo Shoot and Phone Jack   68
Copy Room Encounter   71
Hall Duty Debate   72
Chapter 7: Reflection Questions   74
Suggested Reading   74

8   75
Scheduling Will Not Be a Problem   75
Go Bigger, Not Smaller   77
Ready, Set, Go! Sort of . . .   78
Chapter 8: Reflection Questions   80
Suggested Reading   80

9   81
Circuit Test   81
Our Scary Visitor   82
A Reason They Call Us Lab Rats   85
Back to Camp   86
Learning "A Lesson"   87
A Rainbow Appears   90
Chapter 9: Reflection Questions   91
Suggested Reading   92

IV: Deeper Learning   **93**

   10   **95**
      Born for This Job   95
      First Day   96
      One Tumbleweed   99
      A Day in the Life   99
      A Role Model, Please?   103
      Chapter 10: Reflection Questions   105
      Suggested Reading   105

   11   **107**
      Listening and Reloading   107
      The Art of Thinking Together   108
      Mediating   111
      Collision with Z.   113
      You Can't Make Me   114
      A Culture of "Yeah, but . . ."   116
      Chapter 11: Reflection Questions   117
      Suggested Reading   118

   12   **119**
      Six Months Later   119
      A Dream Coming True   120
      Growing into Your Own True Self   122
      Café Wednesday   123
      Unnatural Behavior   125
      Standardized Children   125
      Chew Gum and Don't Stay with the Group   128
      Chapter 12: Reflection Questions   128
      Suggested Reading   129

   13   **131**
      A Backyard Cookout   131
      Bad Review   133
      Lifer   135
      Chapter 13: Reflection Questions   136
      Suggested Reading   136

V: Evolve   **137**

   14   **139**
      Twenty-Six Again   139
      Rookie   140
      Six Years Later   141
      My New Schooling   143
      Chapter 14: Reflection Questions   145
      Suggested Reading   145

15   147
    It's Okay to Ask a Question   147
    Anguished English   149
    Whatever you say, Prof   151
    Chapter 15: Reflection Questions   153
    Suggested Reading   154

16   155
    Skillful Teaching   155
    Being Blunt   156
    The Idealist Realist   159
    Migrating Online with Video and Audio   161
    Chapter 16: Reflection Questions   164
    Suggested Reading   165

17   167
    Messing with Peoples' Beliefs   167
    Beliefs Fight Back   169
    Three Steps Forward   172
    Two Steps Back   173
    Chapter 17: Reflection Questions   174
    Suggested Reading   174

18   175
    Trouble   175
    Not on the Test   177
    Chapter 18: Reflection Questions   178
    Suggested Reading   178

VI: Big Picture   179
19   181
    Beat Goes On   181
    School as Contested Space   182
    Do the Math   184
    Chapter 19: Reflection Questions   185
    Suggested Reading   185

20   187
    Corner Bar   187
    Endless Fields of Corn   188
    Balance?   189
    Chapter 20: Reflection Questions   191
    Suggested Reading   191

21   193
    Ladder Up a Wall   193
    Ready Enough   195
    Anxiety Dream   198

Chapter 21: Reflection Questions 199
Suggested Reading 199

Foreword

I read it once and sat back in awe. So I read it again.

I could write a book in response because so much of what Nehring has written in *Why Teach?* parallels my own life—and yet in ways that are fascinatingly different. We both entered teaching accidentally and with quite a few prejudices about "teachers" as a class of people. I believe mine were even worse because I accidentally became an early childhood classroom teacher.

All the "types" of educators he describes were part of the landscape, and it took me some time to acknowledge that the very characteristics that so annoyed me in too many of my colleagues were in fact what the institution demanded, brought forth. Unlike them, I was an adult (mid-30s) when I came upon this strange profession with all the habit of mind and manner that made me assume certain "privileges" were due me. I wasn't accustomed to being treated shabbily from the time I entered school until adulthood. Such treatment has its impact; sometimes it creates amazing and fiercely independent fighters or loners—and sometimes it undermines all such potential.

In my two years as a substitute teacher in Chicago I discovered that there was a whole subset of teachers one rarely encountered in the teacher's lounge. They eschewed all contact with adults and built their lives around amazing classrooms where they could create a world of their own and share it with their lucky students. (These are the first victims of the new reforms.)

While reading the book, I recognized Jim's ambivalence—was teaching a way to change the world or just a way to respond to the youngsters in front of us as best we could? If we didn't take the latter seriously, the former was just chutzpah. The best way to change the world might well be quite otherwise—organizing communities and unions, campaigning, writing books, becoming president. Being "change agents" of people seemed to me to be essentially disrespectful and couldn't be the driving force for a lifetime of teaching any more than it could be for parenting.

But the desire to "scale up" one's new ideas, spread them to others, is inevitable. At least for people like Jim and me. We both kept ourselves open to what would come next. And most of the "nexts" fell into our laps unexpectedly.

We encountered each other, as some may already realize, through Ted Sizer and the Coalition of Essential Schools. In 1984, I started a secondary school in East Harlem with Ted's help, as he was starting the Coalition. Here, I discovered, was a man whose perspective on secondary education matched mine on K-6 schooling. In fact, his vision of a good education was, like mine, an extension of a good old-fashioned playful kindergarten—which is where I began.

When Jim was joining the Parker School, I was opening a K-8 school in Boston. Ted and Nancy Sizer were going through the same growing pains launching Parker as I was launching Mission Hill. Though the communities and age groups we served differed, we learned a lot from each other and visited and talked those first few years. We were determined to not assume that the differences in the socio-economics and race of our students and their families required different "methods"—although I think we were also conscious that the differences were profound and important and required attention. I think that our commonalities and our differences strengthened both our endeavors.

I thought about these facts of life as I read Jim's account—and realized that his way of telling the stories made it unnecessary to constantly acknowledge our differences. He brought me into the picture so fully that I didn't need a translator.

Luck may come more easily to the well prepared, but luck surely was on both of our sides. The question facing both of us now is how to figure out what it would take to depend less on luck to have such lucky lives as we have had.

As you read *Why Teach? Notes and Questions from a Life in Education,* I think you'll realize that we're witnessing a rebirth of some of the spirit that led us both into teaching and that helped us invent new ways to imagine how it could be reconfigured on behalf of both democracy and the simple humanity of young people. Reading it with others, as his post chapter queries might suggest, would surely be in keeping with the book's underlying message—being part of a community of learners is in itself a way to learn, and to uncover the thread underlying your life's path.

—Debbie Meier

Deborah Meier spent fifty years in K-12 urban public schools as a teacher—including being the "principal" teacher. She received a MacArthur fellowship in 1989 for her work in reinventing what public education could be. She wrote several books about her experiences and is co-chair of the Coalition of Essential Schools and of Save Our Schools and on the editorial board of Dissent, The Nation, *and the* Harvard Education Letter.

Acknowledgments

First and foremost, I am grateful to my teachers. I have had many over the years. Some were assigned the role because I took a class. Others were co-workers, senior colleagues, or friends of friends who appeared in my life at the right moment, took an interest, and provided guidance and inspiration

In the project that became this book, I am grateful to the Fulbright Program of the U.S. Department of State and the United Kingdom Fulbright Commission. Though the award I received was for the purpose of conducting educational research in Northern Ireland, living abroad provided a crucial psychic distance from my homeland and my accustomed work. In Belfast, I am grateful to the Governors and staff of the Linen Hall Library for providing a haven for intellectual life outside the restricting walls of the university.

Back home, I am grateful to Maureen Stanton, colleague in the English Department at UMass Lowell who provided writerly guidance. My thanks go also to Sarah Jubar at Rowman and Littlefield. At a time when book editors are called upon to manage more than edit, Sarah continues to perform the central task with care and a fine sensitivity to language and narrative structure. I am grateful also to my Sutherland sisters— Peggy, Donna, and Karen—who always manage to provide useful feedback despite my standard request to *just read it and say it's great*.

Finally, words on a page cannot communicate the shaping power of my family in everything I do. They constitute the core of who I am and, without them, anything I might produce would be less than it is. Thank you, Anna, Abbie, Becca, and Laurie.

Introduction

INDOOR WORK

Two months out of college, I was living with my parents on Cape Cod, digging ditches, hanging sheetrock, and laying linoleum. After four years of writing papers, it was—surprisingly—satisfying work. You could see progress. It yielded results. But summer turned to autumn, and autumn turned to bitter New England winter. Manual labor was suddenly no longer fun. That's when teaching quite serendipitously appeared as appealing indoor work. I could stay warm while holding kids hostage to only moderate boredom. And I would have summers off. . .

So it was that I entered teaching for the wrong reasons and found, undeservedly, that I loved the classroom, the endless variety of personalities, and the simple affection of my students. I also got an initiation into a system driven by order, efficiency, rules, rewards, and punishment. I wanted to change that system.

This is how my story begins. The particulars are unique, but the questions I faced, then and over the years since, are relevant to people everywhere: Do you find a vocation by luck or by choice? When do you assimilate and when do you resist? What can you change? What can't you change? How do you keep growing?

I began my quest to change the education system after five years of teaching by writing a book. To my surprise, it was published *and* got good reviews. It was also banned in Idaho for challenging conservative norms. Based on the ideas in the book, I founded a school that became controversial even before it opened. I learned how the system works relentlessly to reject innovation, but the school prevailed and became a haven for learning that honored curiosity and nurtured the minds and hearts of its students.

Several years went by. Then, invited one spring weekend for a friendly visit, I suddenly and unexpectedly found myself the principal of a brand new progressive charter school. I uprooted my young family from New York and moved to a small town in Massachusetts.

Charter schools were new on the scene in the 1990s. Controversy swirled around our school. Some said it was the answer to a broken system. Some demonized us as a right-wing conspiracy. Others dismissed us as a hippie commune. For many parents struggling to raise their adolescent kids, our school was a beacon and a lifesaver.

Our school was by all measures a success, but it was just one school. I wanted to change *the system*.

I was offered a job in the school of education at the University of Massachusetts, and I reinvented myself as an assistant professor. Here was a post from which I could leverage broad change through research, consulting, policy work, and a platform that commanded attention. Or so I thought. Somewhere along the way to tenure and with the good luck of a Fulbright research award, it dawned on me that there was no more magic in the world of higher education than there was in any other point in the system.

As I reflect on thirty-plus years in education, I am struck by a realization about work that transcends every job I ever held. It turns out you don't find meaning by asking "where do I make a difference?" You find it simply by doing well whatever work you are given, because in the end, your greatest point of leverage for social change is always wherever you happen to be.

This truth, at once simple and profound, took me decades to find. I had to try my hand at almost every job in my chosen field, plus a few others. *Why Teach? Notes and Questions from a Life in Education* takes readers on a journey inside our educational system.

This book is intended as a good read, the kind that entertains *and* makes you consider the importance of education. It's also intended, more specifically, for teachers and anyone who aspires to teach. If you are reading this book for a course or professional development group, some lively discussion could result after responding to the Reflection Questions at the end of each chapter. You can also read related books I recommend under "Suggested Reading," including many that withstand the test of time.

HOW THIS BOOK CAME TO BE

So, what is this book? Random notes, spotty recollections, and a collection of queries? As I began to consider this book, I started thinking about the many powerful moments I experienced in thirty years of teaching. I wrote two hundred and fifty pages this way over the course of one year. I wrote a page a day, five days a week, producing over fifty disconnected fragments.

Then I took my cue from the world of social science research, a world in which I found myself immersed since becoming a professor at mid-career, after twenty-five years as a secondary teacher and occasional school leader. While I could not say in advance what patterns and themes would emerge from the fragments of my reconstructed past, I felt certain that patterns and themes were there for the finding if I first wrote the pages, then read them as dispassionately as I could.

This process is a rip-off of something social scientists call *grounded theory,* in which the researcher makes careful observations then culls the transcript for patterns and themes with few assumptions. Though this book is not research and it is not social science, it is, as a personal narrative, a search for patterns. Occasionally, while writing the fragments, I was hit with a thrill of panic that maybe there would be no patterns, that my work life, when it was all laid out, would just be so many random bits. More often, my writing was sustained by a wavering but durable belief that something positive and useful would result from all these pages.

THE HEART OF IT ALL

Here is what I discovered as the manuscript evolved: There is a mystery at the center of teaching, like the hard-to-track energy that physicists tell us runs between subatomic particles. This energy, more than the particles themselves, defines matter. There is an energy that runs between a teacher and his or her students, which, more than the teacher or the students, defines teaching.

The powerful draw of this mystery is regularly confirmed by the legions of accountants, engineers, computer salespeople, and bankers who leave lucrative jobs at mid-career for less money and long hours in order to teach. Teaching is fundamentally mysterious because it is fundamentally relational in the way that Martin Buber, the Jewish mystic philosopher, talked about the mystery of the *I-thou* relationship.

When you and I communicate with one another (I and thou), we summon and enter into a transcendent, shared reality. This reality ceases to exist when our communication ceases. We return to the mundane reality of I-it, the reality in which I survey a world of objects. The mysterious nature of teaching explains why career veterans stammer when you ask them about why they still love their work. Ask and you are liable to get a completely unsatisfactory response: *I make a difference. I share what I love. It's important work.*

People write books about their work lives. I've read memorable accounts of the work life of a fisherman, a carpenter, a physician, an attorney, and, notably, the poet, Donald Hall, who begins his short and powerful book, *Life Work,* with the blunt declaration, "I've never worked a day in my life."

Though I have worked almost every day of my adult life, what draws me in to such a book is a voice that is true and a story that is honest. Work is an appealing subject because it is something, despite Mr. Hall's wry assertion, we all share. Reading about other people's work lives helps us put in perspective our own lot in the world of work. *They, too, have faced bitter failure and moments of triumph. Like us, they've experienced doubt and regret.*

But if I catch the whiff of a formula, my attention will drift. And if the story feels rooted more in some cultural trope than the lived experience of the author, the book will sink in the course of several evenings to the bottom of the little heap of books that rests on my bedside table. So the goal, in constructing this account of my work life, was no more and no less than to be true and to be honest. Events in this book are as I remember them. Names of some people and places have been changed with identifying features altered.

This book reconstructs a journey. A journey has a quest. My quest, which I became fully aware of only after laying out the many memories that comprise this book, has been to find the greatest point of leverage from which I can make a positive impact on my students and the system in which my students must flourish. As a teacher, leader, founder, professor, activist, consultant, researcher, writer, I've discovered a central paradox: my greatest point of leverage is always, exactly, wherever I happen to be.

This book is a story and a manifesto, a quest and a meditation. It is intended to challenge the mind and nourish the soul. It certainly has done that in the writing. I hope it does so in the reading.

I

Entry

ONE

DITCH OF DISTINCTION

My first year of teaching was an adventure characterized by periods of complete and utter confusion, disbelief, self-doubt, and ultimately, as the year wore on, an emerging sense of who I was and who I might become as a teacher and a person. I wish I could lay claim to a longstanding passion for teaching that preceded my entry into the field, or a generational legacy of teachers reaching back to my great grandmother, or a gripping tale of a disturbed adolescence that led me on a quest to right the wrongs that had befallen me so no other child would ever have to endure them. The simple truth is that I landed, almost accidentally, in teaching many years ago.

I was drawn to teaching because I grew to dislike working outdoors through the New England winter. Teaching was a pathway in from the cold. Literally. The story began quite innocently my very first summer after finishing college when I returned home to Cape Cod, uncertain of my next move.

I'd just graduated from the University of Virginia with High Distinction. My first job was digging a ditch that would bring water and electricity to an outbuilding (the shed) that my parents wanted to upgrade to guest quarters. As the digging got underway, I enjoyed the labor and its tangible result: The more I dug, the bigger and deeper the hole became. After four years writing papers, this felt like satisfying work.

By the end of the first day, my ditch was already past the deck off the back of the house, which meant I'd gone just over twelve feet. I was sweaty and covered with dirt—on my clothes, under my fingernails, dusting my arms and face. I quit at 5 p.m., showered, sat down to dinner with a big appetite, and slept the night through like a rock at the bottom of the ocean. I rose the next morning exultant in thoughts of the day ahead. More ditch, more dirt, more labor, more progress. By the end of the second day, I was nearly halfway across the backyard. By the fourth day, I began to feel sad, with just fifteen feet to the foundation of the shed. I was done with the task before noon on Friday.

As summer turned to fall, my college friends scattered, one by one, to purposeful career paths. One became an apprentice architect with a firm that designed schools. Another, an engineer, wrote me a letter about how he was working at a Navy shipyard drawing the bolt that holds the rudder to the hull of a submarine. Another enrolled in business school. I decided to stay the winter on Cape Cod.

I worked for my father as a laborer in his home renovation business, occupying the third floor bedroom under the eaves where I'd slept as a child. Work through the autumn was fine. I was learning practical things like how to lay a linoleum floor, how to frame a house, how to paint windowpanes so the muntin gets covered right to the edge without any paint going onto the glass. Then winter came.

There were the one-shot jobs: fixing the anemometer on a neighbor's roof, moving a cord of wood from one side of a yard to another. Soon I grew tired of outdoor work. So, unwilling to endure without complaint, I'd started to do something about it, somewhat impulsively, but with a kind of wavering determination.

TIME TO MOVE ON

On March 15, 1981, I received two letters in the mail that set my life on a new path, one from Brown University, the other from a prominent Boston-based publisher. How it came to be that those two letters got written and then posted, and then arrived on the very same day is a testament to random coincidence and a reminder that choice, as much as we cling to a belief in it, is at least partly an illusion, a wishful narrative we construct in hindsight to bolster our own tenuous feeling of control over the events of our lives.

Working outside, I'd realized my mind was going flat like soda left out on the kitchen counter. As much as the labor provided physical satisfaction, I craved intellectual stimulation. In the fall, I'd signed up for an intro to anthropology course at UMass Boston and took the bus one day a week, working in the renovation business the rest of the time. Anthropology, I had recently decided, held all the answers to life's big questions: human origins, social behavior, the unity of all humankind.

One day on campus near the end of the term, I saw a tear-off ad for a master of arts in teaching degree at Brown University. "Become a Teacher in One Year." Working hard labor, living at home with my parents, while convenient, was growing tiresome; I was restless. A teacher gets a salary. A salary means you can live on your own. Teaching is a portable career. Every town in America has at least one school. Teachers have lots of vacations. I could move to Vermont, buy an old run-down farm, fix it up during the summer—I was learning a few things about hammers and sheetrock after all.

If I got tired of teaching, I could start a local newspaper, run for office. I could write poems and essays in a sunny little attic outfitted with sky-lights while looking over the morning mist rising from my fields, a steaming cup of coffee within easy reach. This was appealing, and it was all possible. One year.

I reached for the tear-off post card, filled it out, and dropped it in the mailbox before I left campus. Shortly, I put together the application that arrived in the mail. While I was at it, I applied to another teaching program at Colgate University. My future was in motion. I began scanning the *Boston Globe* "Vermont Real Estate" section and was pleased to see that farms could be had for cheap—every Sunday.

Christmas came and went. I was writing more. Winter energized me. The idea of being a teacher had opened my eyes to getting a job worthy of a college degree. Why wait for Brown and Colgate, I thought. I applied for an editorial assistant job at the *Cape Codder*, a weekly newspaper. The ad said they wanted someone who understood "the vagaries of Cape Cod." The serious-looking, energetic man with gray hair who interviewed me looked like he was sitting down for the first time in five hours. He scanned my one page resume and asked, "What is Koine Greek?" which I had listed under "Languages," after German and Spanish.

"It's the original language of the New Testament," I chirped.

Interviewing, at least, had whet my appetite for the search. There were all sorts of possibilities. I decided, for no particular reason, that the world of publishing was my true calling, specifically, working for some venerable Boston book publisher. Several weeks of searching yielded no jobs, but Addison-Wesley, the textbook publisher, needed sales reps. That could be a foot in the door, I thought. I'd start as a sales rep and move into the editorial department. I sent in my resume and shortly was called for an interview. I was called back for another. I got a haircut.

One evening, Colgate University called. The nice lady on the phone said, "We are very interested in you." I said I had changed my mind, and we said goodbye. My father, who was sitting at the kitchen table when the call came in, said, "Are you sure you want to let that option go?" I was being impulsive. My father recognized it. But at the time, I was singularly focused on whatever plan was currently in motion, not a plan I'd made two months before.

Back at Addison-Wesley, I spent a morning shadowing a sales rep as she visited college professors. At Bridgewater State College we saw a man in the sociology department in a three-piece suit who had a framed Harvard Ph.D. degree on the wall. He seemed stiff, and I wondered if it stemmed from vague disappointment that his Harvard degree had landed him only at the local state college. He had two pens neatly arranged in his breast pocket. He did not adopt any of our textbooks.

Leslie, the sales rep, looked maybe five years older than me. She looked like someone I might have met in "Survey of English Lit" class who was not really interested in literature, who was clicking through the requirements for the English major and had her eyes on a life plan that included a fast moving career in business. All morning, she was polite and on schedule, like the UPS man delivering so many packages per hour.

Still, I thought, I could probably do this, but I might not do it quite like her. She asked me at one point if I wanted to lead one of the office visits on our schedule. I declined, not sure what I'd say about the textbooks I knew nothing about. Plus, I wasn't keen on interrupting any of these professors in the middle of their office work.

I was called back for a third and then a fourth interview. I met the national sales manager, who wore a t-shirt and Converse All Stars sneakers. Everybody looked like they were having fun, and they didn't have to work outdoors.

Three weeks passed, and then two letters arrived.

Out by the mailbox, I looked at the letters: one from Addison-Wesley and the other from Brown University. The one from Addison-Wesley said, roughly, *thank you for interviewing, we have reached a decision, and we have decided not to offer you a position. We ask that you not apply, again, for a position at Addison-Wesley now or in the future.* I went a little numb with that. The word "not" was all I needed to see, but the "don't apply again" made me feel especially inadequate.

I tore open the other envelope, pulled out the letter, and unfolded it. *Pleased to inform you* was the first phrase that registered. I took in the first paragraph. I was being admitted. This was an admission letter to a master's program at Brown University.

While absorbing that, I moved into a second paragraph where I read the phrase "tuition scholarship." I re-focused and read carefully. I was being offered a scholarship for the cost of the full tuition. I grabbed all the mail from the box and walked up to the house. I told my mother. She said, "The writing is on the wall." I thought, Okay, I'll go to Brown. Why not? I like campus life. I know how to "do" college. I could take lots of anthropology courses and uncover the meaning of everything. I could learn how to teach. That's where my happy go-back-to-college fantasy entered a fog. What do you do in a learn-how-to-teach class? Is teaching a subject for which you can even have a course?

HOLDING KIDS HOSTAGE

Brown University wanted me to visit school classrooms before starting my program. During the March drizzle season I began to do so. I contacted the principal of the local high school and shortly found myself in the back of Mr. Conklin's ninth grade U.S. History class.

Mr. Conklin was teaching with vigor about Teddy Roosevelt and the idea of national parks that Roosevelt championed. He showed a filmstrip featuring Yosemite, and led a discussion with the class. Mr. Conklin was all energy and bustle. His students politely looked on. One kid in the back row had his head down next to a stack of textbooks. I looked at the rest of the students, who looked bored and zoned out, like zombies.

Is this what it meant to be a teacher? It was definitely better than hawking textbooks, but not by much. I wondered, what if the kids were all energy and bustle while Mr. Conklin looked on? I had no clue how to make textbook sales more palatable, but what about teaching? There might be a better way to go about this task, and I might figure it out at Brown University.

I felt a pulse of hope. Meanwhile, I was perched happily in a warm and dry space away from the March cold. I settled in like Mr. Conklin's students and enjoyed the day.

The rainy season relented and the weather turned warm. We cruised into summer, and shortly it was time for me to head to Providence to start my exciting new life. I packed some clothes and took with me my only two major possessions: a blue Volvo wagon that I bought during the winter with 110,000 miles on the odometer and a blue four-drawer file cabinet I'd picked up at a yard sale. I was excited to learn about teaching.

Hammering nails had grown dull and predictable. To install a kitchen floor, you put down the underlayment, nail it eight inches square, cut the linoleum, apply adhesive, lay it out, cut the quarter round, and run it around the perimeter. Done. I could get cleaner with my cuts and faster overall, but that was pretty much it. I thought about the kid drooling at the back on Mr. Conklin's classroom. Now there was an interesting challenge.

So with matching car and file cabinet, I went off to learn how to teach.

CHAPTER 1: REFLECTION QUESTIONS

1. How do you find a vocation? Is it by choice or chance? What role do choice and chance play in this chapter? What's your story?
2. How does a liberal arts graduate make a successful transition from college to work?

3. Are the liberal arts a good foundation for a career? Is college principally about securing a career? Given the limited vocational options, is a liberal arts degree elitist?
4. What draws Jim Nehring to teaching in this chapter? What draws any person to teaching? Are there good reasons, bad reasons? Do they matter? What reasons have stood behind your vocational choices?
5. Are the reasons that draw you into a profession the reasons that keep you there? What were the reasons behind your career choices (to the extent you chose)? Did those reasons hold up after you entered your field?
6. There are push and pull factors in the selection of a vocation. How do they play out for Jim Nehring in this chapter? How have they played out in your life?

SUGGESTED READING

There is no lack of how-to books for choosing a vocation. Just check the careers section at any bookstore. However, if you want something that gets at the deeper issues involved in major life choices, try Albert Bandura's *Self Efficacy: The Exercise of Control,* which explains how people are both influenced by and have influence over their environment. Consider also, Gail Sheehy's *Passages: Predictable Crises of Adult Life.* First published in 1984, this seminal work remains relevant across the decades.

TWO

TEACHING AND TELLING

Alastair Hollingberry wore a cape—an actual cape ala Sherlock Holmes—which, even at Brown University in 1981, was considered over the top. And he smoked a pipe. He taught philosophy and was the senior professor of the Education Department. We were all afraid of Hollingberry. But he had a softer side. He'd show up at graduate student parties, and I ran into him at one.

"So, Nehring, how are you justifying your existence these days?" asked Hollingberry, swirling his chardonnay. Everyone else was drinking Narragansett Beer.

Unsure of myself, I took the question at face value. How else should I take it, after all? When Hollingbery asked you a question like that, he meant it.

"I'm learning to be a teacher so that I may make a positive contribution to society. I am learning that it's the kind of work that I enjoy such that I am in the happy circumstance of doing good while enjoying what I do."

Hollingberry arched an eyebrow and regarded me. "And what is it that you 'enjoy' about teaching? Is it the snot that runs down the faces of your young charges?"

"I like the moment."

"The moment?"

"I like the moment of teaching, the connection between me and my students. Martin Buber's I-Thou." I'd read the Jewish mystic philosopher one winter between semesters when I was in college. Buber said that when *you* and *I* enter into a relationship, we transcend the mundane world of "I-it"—a world in which *I* survey objects—and *we* encounter a transcendent reality. This made sense to me.

Hollingberry tipped his virtual hat to me. "Cheers," he added and turned away. He was a character, and he made us think. The moment of teaching is something I was only beginning to learn about. We'd done a brief teaching stint with high school students who came to the Brown campus for enrichment. I found it nowhere short of amazing that they all turned their faces toward me and listened. They seemed hungry for attention in a way I was to learn is nearly universal among adolescents, and I was eager for their approval, perhaps too eager in those early days. The connections we made were confirmation that my nearly accidental departure for a career in teaching might have set me, after all, on the right path.

Alastair Hollingberry taught "Philosophical Analysis of Educational Concepts." He corrected you if you said casually, "Philosophy of Education." The class met on Monday afternoon in a lecture room in the back of Sayles Hall. The space radiated Edwardian formality, which suited Hollingberry.

"Kiminsky, what is material?" Hollingberry abruptly started the class. Entering through a side door, he noted the students who were already at their seats, and he asked the first question of the day before putting down his briefcase.

"Material is subject matter," Danny Kiminsky replied. Hollingberry rarely addressed anyone by first name.

Hollingberry paused in the midst of taking off his cape. "What's that?" he asked, and resumed getting settled.

"Subject matter is the stuff the class is studying," said Kiminsky sitting up a little straighter.

"The *stuff* the class is studying." Hollingberry repeated, his voice trailing off as he peered into his open brief case, which he had set on a chair by the lecturn.

"Nehring, what do you make of that?" He pulled a manila folder out of the old leather bag and dropped it on the lecturn with a slap, timed as an exclamation mark to his own sentence.

"Umm . . ." I said. Hollingberry sniffed, standing at the lecturn, eyes straight ahead.

"Material," I began again, "is the reason the student and the teacher are meeting. It is the focus of their relationship."

"And how," Hollingberry replied, "does one distinguish *that* from purpose?" He paused, and then called, "Parato?" Parato was studying to be an English teacher.

"Purpose," Parato began crisply, "is the reason the student and the teacher meet, and material is whatever mediates the purpose. For example, your purpose as teacher today is for us, the students, to distinguish among the essential educational concepts. The material is the concepts themselves: student, teacher, material, and purpose."

Hollingbery sniffed again. "You think you're smart, Parato?" Hollingberry let loose a hint of a smile as he returned his gaze to his notes.

Every class was like this. All last names, Socratic questioning, and cold-calling. Hollingberry kept us alert, and he taught us fundamentals, like teaching versus telling.

"What is the difference between teaching and telling?" he began one class. "If I *tell* you a story, am I *teaching*? Bronstein?"

Michael Bronstein was probably the quickest mind in the class. He began, "If you are telling me a story, you are conveying something, information. I may choose to listen or not."

"If you are teaching, do I have no choice but to listen?" Hollingberry replied.

"You do, but it's different."

"What is the difference between teaching and telling?" Hollingberry asked.

Another student, Lauren Sullivan, tried a response. "The difference lies in the purpose. If I am telling you something, the purpose is for me to say the words. If I say the words, then I have told, regardless of whether you have heard."

"And teaching?" Hollingberry continued.

There was a silence.

I tried: "Teaching is not an act. It is a purpose that stands behind an act. If I tell you a story and my purpose is to teach, then it matters whether you listen, and it matters what you do with the story I tell you. If my purpose is for you to be able to provide an interpretation of the story, then I might ask you a question about the story before I tell it and say that I'll expect an answer after the story is told."

Hollingberry: "What then is teaching?"

Bronstein: "It's an intention."

Hollingberry: "You're with Nehring, eh? *Any* intention? If I intend to jump out the window, am I teaching?"

Bronstein: "It is an intention to produce change in the mind of an individual."

Hollingberry: "How is that different from brainwashing? Or advertising?"

Bronstein: "It's not coercion. And it is for growth and learning. And it has the well-being of the individual in mind."

I'd never really thought much about teaching before coming to Brown. I didn't think of it as a subject that you study, like English or history. I'd thought teaching maybe belonged to some lesser tier of academic departments, which a friend during college described as "codification of the obvious." It was something that a smart person would just sort of figure out. How hard could it be?

And yet, there I was. Though education may have been primarily a path in from the cold, I was learning that this particular form of indoor work required skill.

STUDENT WILL BE ABLE TO . . .

Hollingberry built up my philosophical chops. Annabel McCart actually taught me how to teach. Annabel was petite, earnest, organized, and kept everything in a three-ring binder. Snap! It's open. Snap! It's shut. She taught us social studies methods and showed us a template for planning a lesson that helped me begin to appreciate the fact that teaching didn't just happen, it wasn't something that smart people just figured out. I did not appreciate at the time I was a student that her recipe was an amalgam of ideas developed in universities and classrooms over the last half-century. I knew only that it worked. Her lesson planning had four parts.

1. Introduction: an activity designed to raise questions and pique student interest in the material to be studied.
2. Focus: the teacher reveals the purpose of the lesson and what the learning objectives for the lesson are.
3. Development: a series of activities in which students gain familiarity with the material.
4. Application: students take the concepts and skills they have just learned and use them in a different situation in order to cement their understanding and demonstrate that they have, in fact, learned them.

It turns out Annabel McCart's method is a durable recipe that can be used to turn almost any topic into a lesson plan that works. I clung to it like a life raft during the tsunami called student teaching, which was about to arrive on the tranquil shores of my graduate student life.

At the heart of McCart's method are the objectives. She said to always start with objectives: what is it that you want your students to know and be able to do at the end of the lesson. It is crucial, Annabel also said, to state your objectives in behavioral terms, that is, to use words that call for an observable act: the student will be able to *describe* how the 1918 flu epidemic began and how it spread worldwide; the student will be able to *explain* the dilemma between the need to safeguard public health and the need to preserve individual liberties; the student will be able to *apply* knowledge about the 1918 flu epidemic to a different public health problem. "The student will be able to. . . ." SWBAT became our shorthand.

"Annabel, How about this: 'students will understand three causes of the Great Depression'?" a fellow student ventured during class one afternoon when we were practicing our SWBATs. McCart's class took place in a small, whitewashed room on the top floor of Simon Eissner House. Nine of us sat at welded desk and chair units in a small circle. The space was clinical and utilitarian, which somehow suited McCart in the same way the ornate lecture hall suited Hollingberry.

"How will you know they understand the three causes?" asked Annabel, unsnapping one of her many binders at a table covered with notebooks. It felt like the whole room jumped every time one of her binders snapped.

"Because they will talk about them on the test."

"What specifically will you ask them to do on that test?" She removed a three-hole-punched paper from the binder.

"I'll ask them to name the three causes."

"So, think about how to construct your objective with that in mind." Snap. The binder shut, and everyone in the room made a little jump.

"The student will be able to name three causes of the Great Depression."

"Better, but if they're *naming* something, they are just repeating what they heard, right?" Annabel studied her binders as though trying to remember which one contained the paper she was looking for.

"I suppose," said my classmate.

"Is that what you want them to do?" Snap. Another binder opened.

"I guess I'd want them to be able to put it in their own words."

"Okay, so what's a verb that's a little more open-ended than 'name' and lets students use their own words?" Here, Annabel paused from her paper removal project, with her fingers poised on the rings of the binder. She fixed her gaze on her student in a gentle but insistent manner.

"I give up."

"How about 'identify'?" McCart offered.

McCart demanded precision from her students. She insisted not only that we be clear in our own minds about what we teach, but that we have a way of knowing whether our students actually learned. And the only way we would know is if the students demonstrated this in some observable way: naming, identifying, describing, explaining, etc. That's why she wanted our objectives stated in strictly behavioral terms: "Student Will Be Able To . . ."

It is accurate to say she drilled this into us. But the real test lay ahead. I had to take all the Hollingberry philosophy and all the McCart teaching methods and somehow use them as my survival tools during a semester of student teaching with real, live, scary high school students.

REAL STUDENTS

Ken was going to let me teach anthropology, which he said was the only high school anthropology course in the state of Rhode Island. It was 1982. I felt hugely privileged. Ken, my newly assigned mentor teacher at Alewife High School in Warwick, had designed the class himself and taught it as an elective. I'd recently decided, based on one course at UMass Boston, that anthropology was my true calling and the path to understanding all human activity.

I would be teaching the class five days a week to twenty-six high school juniors and seniors. Ken said he preferred that I take over the class right from the start so that the students would see me as their teacher, not Ken's student teacher. There was a textbook, which I read and re-read. I found several other introductory books in the library. I learned about the division between physical anthropology (the study of human origins) and cultural anthropology (the study of deep patterns of human behavior in groups). I was fascinated by the careers of Louis Leakey and Richard Leakey, who explored in east Africa during the "digging season" then went back home to England to lecture. I was intrigued by cultural universalities such as religion, government, economics, social ranking, and how features common to all cultures found particular expression in each. I liked taking apart words into their ancient Greek components: Australopithecus—southern ape; anthropology—man, study of.

With a month of reading over Christmas vacation, I was working hard to convince myself that I was an expert. Had Indiana Jones made his appearance in popular culture, I would have bought a bomber jacket, hat, and whip.

Several weeks before my first day of teaching, I began obsessing about my first lesson. I wanted my students to have a great experience. They should become as fascinated as I was by fossil discoveries in Olduvai Gorge, the caves in Lascaux, France, and remote cultures in the Amazon River Basin and Central Africa, isolated from industrial society. They could be struck with the same disarming realization that as remote as they were, such people are still, fundamentally, like us.

But I couldn't just *tell* them all these things. The goal was for my students to be active, out of their seats, handling objects, looking at displays, figuring stuff out. In my teaching methods class, we had studied the MACOS Curriculum—"Man: A Course of Study," a well-informed program, popular in the 1970s that engaged students with questions and problems. That's the feel I wanted for my anthropology course.

I started to imagine that the introductory lesson would consist of several stations. At each one there would be objects, images, and text, and students would be prompted with questions. Free to move about the room with the students, I would monitor their work and coach individuals. I began to identify the key ideas students should learn from their first lesson. I photocopied bits of text and images from various books, including the textbook. Materials clustered around several themes and five stations began to emerge. I bought poster board and composed a student handout with instructions and prompts for each station. I typed them up on a ditto master and made copies. Ken looked it over and declared it marvelous.

DAY ONE

My first day, I felt confident and exhilarated. I gave a short introduction about the course and myself to the class, explaining that the real introduction would be an activity. Slowly, students rose from their seats. They began to explore the stations, hesitant at first, touching the objects and looking at pictures. Before long there was a noisy hum as students talked about what they were finding and figuring out.

Laughter erupted from one group of three students. I strolled over and listened as they imagined all the possible ways "australopithecus" might be pronounced. I laughed with them, admitted it was a ridiculous, complicated word, and pointed out that I was not responsible for inventing it, but I could explain it: Australo- southern; pithecus—ape. They nodded with genuine interest and went back to handling artifacts.

I thought about my day with Mr. Conklin, which was the first time I'd been back in a high school classroom since I was a student myself. I'd felt at the time I wanted more, and I wondered if the privilege of indoor work required some trade off. I could work inside as a teacher, but I would have to torture adolescents with deathly boring material. Apparently this was not the case.

My first lesson worked in every way I had imagined. I thought—my career is launched! Except that, when I got home, I had to start thinking about what to do on *Tuesday*. I realized that, in fact, there were four more days in my first week. I had spent two weeks planning one day's lesson.

In the end, I made it through student teaching. Average planning time for a lesson moved quickly from two weeks to a single evening of nearly continuous panic, and pretty soon twenty-four hours felt adequate to prepare a new lesson, with occasional bonus time for sleep. I learned I didn't have to create an entire museum every day in order to engage my students. A few carefully chosen prompts and logical sequencing of small group and whole group work went a long way.

My students *wanted* to learn. They were curious about the world. It was my job to ask the right questions to get them started and identify objectives worthy of their intellectual capacity. Their chairs might be welded to their desks, but *they* didn't have to be welded to their chairs. They were kids, after all, and they wanted to move around. I realized learning could be active.

It also helped that I felt like I didn't know enough about anything to teach it. Better, therefore, to let my students read about it and figure it out themselves. This, it turns out, was a useful deficit because it ensured an approach driven by questions, projects, and just about any form of teaching other than lecture. I can count on two hands the number of times I've lectured in a career of thirty plus years.

IN SEARCH OF A FIRST JOB

Weeks turned to months, and I was beginning to imagine myself a real teacher. Good thing because my year at Brown was rapidly coming to an end. In May, I began looking for a teaching job. My dream of buying a farm in Vermont vanished when I learned that teacher salaries there were unlivable. New York State, on the other hand, had a strong teacher union, and salaries were good.

I considered the Hudson River Valley, which I remembered from visits to my grandparents who lived in Dutchess County, back when I was a kid. For me, growing up near New York City, Dutchess County was upstate. It was *the country* with rolling hills, farms, smoke curling from chimneys, and misty meadows. I imagined scenes from the Hudson River School of painting with its dramatic vistas, sun streaked cloudscapes, and expansive, tawny fields of windblown grass. (Never mind that most of the scenes were not the Hudson River.) It was lodged in my imagination, and I decided it was the place for me.

I blanketed the region's fifty-plus school districts with my resume, inserting a unique address and salutation for each in the form letter on my IBM Selectric typewriter. It was 1982, and the economy was in recession. There were not many teaching jobs to be had, but I got a call back from the Middle Valley Central School District. They needed someone to teach English and Social Studies in their middle school. The job required certification in both subjects, which I had due to a lucky combination of coursework. I interviewed and got the job.

I bought a new car. The Volvo had blown a head gasket crossing the Green Mountains in Vermont and got sold. But I still had my blue file cabinet, which I slid into the back of my shiny new Nissan Sentra. I was off to New York State and my first real teaching job.

CHAPTER 2: REFLECTION QUESTIONS

1. What is teaching? How is it different from telling? From selling? From brainwashing?
2. Did you have a favorite professor? What did you learn from him or her? Did they possess qualities you have tried to emulate?
3. Are there certain essential features for a good lesson plan? What are they?
4. Can you think of a really excellent class in which you were a student? What are the elements of the design that made it so memorable?
5. Is education an academic discipline like history and science and math? If so, why is it sometimes looked down on? If you think it is not a discipline, explain why. If not a discipline, what is it?

6. Can a smart person pick up teaching on their own or does it require training?
7. Is it important to know in advance what you want your students to be able to do by the end of the lesson?
8. Do you have to believe something is important in order to teach it well?
9. Can it be helpful to NOT be an expert in something in order to teach it well? If so, how?

SUGGESTED READING

One of the best books about the basics of teaching is a slim volume first published over fifty years ago. *Basic Principles of Curriculum and Instruction* by Ralph Tyler offers guidance for the creation of a lesson or a whole course of study that has stood the test of time. The most influential contemporary guide for teaching is *Understanding by Design* by Grant Wiggins and Jay McTighe. It draws on Tyler's work, updating it for modern concerns.

Nel Noddings' *Philosophy of Education* provides an excellent introduction to the big questions that surround teaching. For a superb analysis of learning that has yet to be matched nearly a century after it was first published, read John Dewey's *Experience and Education*.

II

Beginner

THREE

WHAT ARE KIDS LIKE?

"Nehring, kids are like dogs; they smell fear," said Ron Johnson, a retired army man, who was the other ninth grade social studies teacher at Middle Valley Middle School. Ron was full of wise sayings, which he generously offered to me. Ron also said, "Learning is not fun. It may at times be pleasant, but it is work. It is mostly drudgery."

This is not the way Hollingberry or McCart or Ken talked about teaching. But two hundred miles from their protective bubble, I was not going to backtalk Ron Johnson. I sensed only, in my first real teaching job, that something in the environment was shifting. I was less conscious that something inside of me was also shifting.

"Kids are like dogs; they smell fear," is a sentence I included in a letter I wrote to Ken. I missed him. I was feeling unsure of myself. Besides his job at Alewife High School, Ken taught part-time at Brown in the Education Department. He was proof that a bonafide schoolteacher could carry into a real classroom the ideas that Hollingberry and McCart talked about. Ken felt to me like an anchor in a storm. But just two months into my journey as a teacher, I was starting to think more like Ron Johnson. My anchor was slipping. Ken didn't write back.

THAT ONE STUDENT

I taught six classes: three sections of ninth grade social studies, two sections of ninth grade English, and one section of eighth grade business because they needed somebody to teach it.

Todd Harper sat at the back of my fifth period English class. At the time, I was using a seating chart, which I relied on too much to manage student behavior. For the challenging group that Todd was a part of, I was never able to keep everyone engaged in the lesson from day to day,

21

and came to view the seating chart as a magical fix. If I just got the arrangement of kids right, all would be well. If I just put easily distracted and verbally impulsive Timothy in between two quiet and serious students, like Jamie and Richard, then Timothy would be neutralized. But then, I'd be using up quiet and serious students and wouldn't have any left for the three other students who did not do well in a classroom setting. Students like Todd Harper.

Todd was tall, slender, and pale. He wore skinny blue jeans, a t-shirt, and well-scuffed army style boots every day, and he sported a chrome chain that ran from the belt loop on his right hip to the rear pocket. Todd cultivated the role of subversive. It is what everyone had come to expect of him and what he thrived on. Failing classes and getting sent to the principal without being shaken was his modus operandi.

In the eyes of many of his peers, Todd was cool. There was apparently no countervailing force at home telling him that while his actions rewarded him with a secure identity in the moment, they had a longer downside in terms of school failure and diminished options just a few years down the road.

This was, sadly, the situation for a number of my students at the Middle Valley Middle School, most from households with little money, little schooling, and a diminished vision for human potential that seemed to get smaller from one generation to the next. These were not proud rural folk who eschewed formal education for the lessons of farm life. They were outcasts from an economy in flux. Their grandparents were farmers whose once prosperous operations slowly fell to ruin as demand and prices for milk declined. Their parents had been reasonably well-paid blue-collar workers in mid-size manufacturing companies who lost their jobs when the factories closed and the owners moved south for lower wages. These were households set up in trailer parks dotting the county where people got by on WIC and AFDC support and occasional work. Homes where there was poverty and anger and too much alcohol and a mean dog tied to a stake out front that barked all day giving a coarse animal voice to the unhappiness that reigned inside. This was not the Yorkshire dales of James Herriott, nor was it a painting from the Hudson River School.

Somehow, Todd Harper ended up in the back row. You would think the front row to be a better location for a student prone to distraction and in need of one-on-one attention. This is what I thought, too, in the early iterations of my not-so-magical seating chart. What I discovered, however, was that the front row provided a stage upon which Todd could perform for the whole class.

"Todd, would you have a seat, please?"

"And what if I say no, Mr. Nehring?"

"Todd, can I please have the papers that your row just passed forward?"

"What papers?"

"Todd, can I help you with that?"

"No, Mr. Nehring. I am beyond help."

By the third or fourth seating chart, I got the idea that if I put Todd in the back of the room, no one would be watching him. This actually worked for about fifteen minutes. Then Todd figured out that he just had to make a bigger scene that would make everyone turn around, and if he did it when I was down front, addressing something else, I would have to call across the length of the classroom.

"Todd, can you please stop that!"

Everyone's head would turn, and Todd would show a surge of delight and make an even bigger act. I was frustrated. I didn't know what to do, and the rest of the class knew it.

Todd's greatest success as classroom subversive came in the spring. I was leading a discussion from the front of the room, when I noticed that Todd was studying something on the floor by his desk. He was seated sideways, and his head was down. He was looking at a spot on the floor between his knees. He wasn't moving. It was the most studious I had ever seen him.

I decided to do nothing about it for the moment, having learned the error of calling for his attention from the front of the room. Soon, I had an opportunity to move to the back of the room after I gave the class a short reading assignment. I got to the last row near Todd's desk. Todd did not move. He gazed at the floor, where I saw a piece of notebook paper. Something dripped onto the paper.

"Todd, what are you doing?"

"Making art."

"Would you please set your art aside and take a look at the reading?"

"No, I will not."

"I see. May I ask what you're doing?"

Todd looked up. "I already said. Making art." When Todd looked up, I had a clear view of the art project. I couldn't believe it.

I crouched low in order to be eye-level with Todd and to exclude others from our conversation since what I was about to say had the potential to rile the whole class.

"Todd," I began softly. "Is that blood?"

It appeared he had pricked his finger and was dripping droplets of blood onto the paper to create a design.

Todd replied, loud enough to foil my private conversation attempt, "Yes, Mr. Nehring, that's blood. That's my blood."

At this, Rhonda Rodenton, who was sitting next to Todd said, "Oh, that is so gross."

Five more heads turned. When they figured out what was going on, there were similar expressions of shock and disgust. This had a ripple effect all the way up the rows so that within a couple seconds the whole

class was astir. Meanwhile, Todd set his gaze back to the floor and returned calmly to his project.

"Todd, I can't let you do this in my classroom."

"That's unfortunate, Mr. Nehring."

"Todd, I think I need to send you to Mr. Costello's office."

"That's cool."

With that, he reached down, scooped up his paper, paused a moment
to gently blow on the surface to dry it, then got up and left the room,
carefully holding his project out in front.

LOSING MY WAY

Memory is unreliable. Here's why. I'm not sure this is how the Todd
Harper episode ended. There's a competing recollection that changes, not
so much the subject of this story, but the teller. Coming out of Brown's
Master of Arts in teaching program, I was steeped in adolescent psychology and principles of pedagogy. I had been transformed in my year there
into a junior social scientist. My aspiration at one point was that, after five
years working in schools, I would return to the university, get my Ph.D.
and then teach in a college of education.

Environment has a way of changing things. At Middle Valley Middle
School, I was suddenly teaching six classes, each with twenty-five to
thirty students, and covering three subjects. Among these six classes were
a good number of fourteen- and fifteen-year olds who didn't especially
want to be sitting at a desk all day. I was exposed to many teachers who
used, shall we say, "shortcuts" in their classroom management style of
which my professors at Brown would likely not have approved.

For example, Mr. Costello, who served as assistant principal, used a
tough guy approach and had a verbal arsenal intended to quickly silence
and reform misbehaving youngsters so they could be quickly re-seated in
whatever classroom they'd just been ejected from. I observed this on
several occasions.

Once, I sent one of my students, Billy, out of the room because he
refused to put away his shotgun, and it was becoming a distraction. (It
wasn't actually a whole shotgun—it was just the stock—minus lock and
barrel—which he was going to re-finish in shop class.) I thought maybe
I'd over-reacted. As soon as class ended, I went to Mr. Costello's office
where Billy was seated just outside the door. Mr. Costello called us both
in. We sat down in chairs across from Mr. Costello's large, uncluttered
desk.

"What did you do now, Billy?" said Mr. Costello.

"Nuthin."

"Don't give me that bull cocky, Billy. Mr. Nehring is an intelligent man, and he would not send you down here for 'nuthin.'" Now, you tell me exactly what happened, and you better make sure you get it right."

With this, Mr. Costello eyed me as if to say, "watch and learn." I sat up straight. Billy continued to slump.

"I guess I was foolin' around, but it wasn't a big deal."

"Listen to me, Billy, and listen good because I am going to tell you what a big deal is." Costello leaned forward, placing his stocky forearms on the desk top. He had a big watch with a chrome band on his left wrist. "I don't care what kind of cock and bull story you come in here with because you have no credibility, you hear me? None at all. If Mr. Nehring tells me you were causing trouble in his class, then that's it. End of story. Now, frankly, I don't need to hear whatever you're going to make up about what you did or did not do because if Mr. Nehring says you did it, then you did it."

This was for my benefit. Mr. Costello was demonstrating that he was *supporting his teachers.* I think I felt more afraid than supported. I was afraid for Billy. I was afraid of having to be like Mr. Costello, but I was thinking, I guess that's what I'm supposed to do.

Mr. Costello continued, "So here's the deal, Billy. You are going back to Mr. Nehring's room tomorrow. You are going to sit there quietly and respectfully. You are going to do as you are told because you know what, Billy?"

Silence from Billy.

"Billy, you look at me when I'm talking to you."

Billy looked up.

"Here's what, Billy. If you screw up again in Mr. Nehring's class, I will have you tossed out of here so fast, it'll make your head spin. Do you understand me, Billy? Billy, you look at me when I'm talking to you."

Billy continues to look at Mr. Costello.

"Are we squared away, Billy? Are we squared away?" Mr. Costello's forearms had crept farther across his desk, his eyes bulging. He looked as if he might just strangle Billy.

"Yeah," Billy muttered tentatively.

"You say, 'Yes, sir,' Billy. I want to hear, 'Yes, sir' from you."

Billy said, "Yes, sir."

"Now get out of my office, and I don't want to see you back here again. Go to your next class. You don't need a pass."

Billy left. I remained, slightly afraid of what might happen next. Mr. Costello said, "Billy's a good kid, he just needs a good swift kick in the butt. You gotta be tough with kids like Billy. It's the only way a bonehead like him gets it, ya know?"

Mr. Costello smiled, leaning back in his chair. I was unnerved by how quickly Mr. Costello switched his tone. It was like he'd been acting. He *was* acting. Did I have to act, too? Mr. Costello wasn't the only one who acted this way with students. It was the same with Mr. Fleisch, the principal, and Ron Johnson, and even Amanda Burke, the seventh grade English teacher. It was a kind of boot camp approach, or at least the kind of boot camp they show in movies with the "tough but fair" sergeant.

I hate to say, but truthfully, my encounter with Todd Harper in the blood-dripping incident may have gone like this:

Rhonda Rodenton says, "Oh that is so gross," at which point I stride briskly to the back of the room and demand of Todd Harper, who has his head between his legs gazing at his handiwork, "What the heck is going on here?"

Todd doesn't make a move. He remains calm, head down.

"Mr. Harper, I asked you a question." I move from demanding into boot camp sergeant mode, which I've been learning from the likes of Mr. Costello and Mr. Johnson. "Harper!" I drop the Mister. "Do you hear me?"

No reaction.

"Harper, if you don't motivate your butt out of that chair right now, I will come down on you like a ton of bricks. I will have your sorry behind kicked out of this school so fast it will make your head spin."

Todd Harper slowly looks up and meets my gaze. "Now get up and step out into the hall with me." I pause for effect. "You and I are going to have a little talk."

Butts, behinds, carcasses, tailbones, and spinning heads. It was discipline by verbal intimidation, military style, and it had seeped into my repertoire, a repertoire which, in my first year of teaching, was not very deep and was easily filled with whatever words the environment provided. This is what the environment provided.

Memory is unreliable. Not because of some technical failing of brain cells, but because it is locked in a struggle with embarrassment. I am embarrassed, looking back, at how easily I was swayed to become someone I fundamentally was not by the behaviors of the educators around me.

Sometimes I want to reconstruct events in a way that's more palatable. The truth is I may have done Todd Harper more harm than good with the "tough guy" approach. I may have simply confirmed his view of the adult world as crude and belligerent. A friend told me once that because we are determined by our environment, he chooses his friends carefully. I love this paradoxical comment because it captures an essential truth.

FINDING MY WAY BACK

The truth is, my teacher persona was completely wet clay. Put me in someone else's classroom and I'd become that person. I'm told that first year teachers are often so completely rattled by the intensity of the experience that they grab at anything that looks like it might work just to get through it. That was me. Ron Johnson, Mr. Costello, and play-acting boot camp discipline looked like it worked, so I grabbed it. Fortunately, however, there were teachers besides Ron and Mr. Costello, teachers who held a fundamentally nobler belief about human capacity that steered clear of boot camp discipline and dog metaphors.

Hank and Roy were buddies. At the time I knew them, they were forty-ish and had been teaching at the Middle Valley Middle School for nearly twenty years. They sat in the teacher's lounge and smoked cigarettes. They were never in a hurry. Students liked them. Hank taught eighth grade English across the hall from me. Between classes, standing by his doorway, he'd greet students as they walked by. Tall, handsome, slow mannered, and ready with a smile.

"Hey, Tony. Yankee's gonna pull out a win?" Hank calls from his classroom door to an approaching crowd. "Huh? What are the odds." Hank chuckles.

Tony, a lanky eighth grader, calls back, "Two to one. Show me your money." The crowd is all smiles and bright eyes as they walk past. Hank's attention turns to a young man entering his room, who is telling Hank something serious. He doesn't have his homework. Hank listens thoughtfully. They turn and enter Hank's classroom. Hank has his arm on the boy's shoulder.

I'm monitoring study hall one day. It's an unusually warm day in early October. Doors and windows are open. I can hear Hank leading his English class across the hall. He is calling names and asking each student if their homework is done. Students answer and most say yes. A few say no.

I wonder, is Hank being easy or is he being a good teacher, giving his students the chance to be truthful? If someone doesn't tell the truth, Hank will find out soon enough, so why not just ask? I decide he's being a good teacher. Later in the same class, I hear Hank leading a discussion about something the class read. "What do you think?" I hear. And, "What do you think about what Megan just said?" There are long pauses between Hank's questions, and I realize the pauses are when students are speaking, whose softer voices I can't hear.

Hank doesn't say much. I hear him call different names. More long pauses. I picture a serious and orderly discussion and engaged students. I learn from Hank all year through the walls and in the halls. It would be logical to ask Hank if I could sit in on his class during my free period, but there's a code among teachers that keeps me from doing so. This code says, what you do in your classroom is your business.

There was also Richard McConnel, a well-liked eighth grade math teacher. I was naturally interested in teachers who were well-liked. If the person was also a good teacher, the pull was that much stronger. The casual glimpses I caught of Richard's teaching suggested he was both. Without thinking much about it, I began to take on his manner.

Richard was gruff. "What's your excuse?" He'd say as a morning greeting to a student. Richard was also understated. If a student was blithely poking his classmate in the next row, Richard would turn calmly toward him, catch his eye, and say, "Conrad." Pause. "Maybe not." Conrad would stop, and Richard would return to teaching.

Richard was, above all else, unflappable. One day, a fight broke out in the hall just outside Richard's classroom between periods. I happened to be walking by just as Richard was intervening. He said nothing. In fact, he did almost nothing. He casually walked (he didn't run) a few steps to where the two boys were pushing each other and simply stood very nearly in the space of their shoving-fight and watched. Richard was tall so he was a looming presence over most of our middle school students, including these two youngsters. It was perhaps Richard's not doing anything besides just standing right there, towering over them, that got the boys' attention and made them pause long enough for Richard to say, "Stop." Pause. "Now." And they did. It was like magic. I wanted to be Richard.

And so I tried. I was gruff. I was calm and unflappable. I even tried to seem taller by standing up straighter and standing closer to students so that, if at all possible, I could look down at them. Here's the thing: it worked. When Billy walked into class one day I said, "What's your excuse?" in the same matter-of-fact way I'd seen Richard use. Billy grunted and then was cooperative during class. I tried to be low key in class, and I found it calmed the students down.

The students' energy, I realized, was generated, at least in part, out of a response to my energy. If I was hyper, jumping around the room, then so were they. If I was calm and low key, they were, too. Eventually, my Richard persona wore off, but I retained the lesson that the energy in the classroom can mirror the energy of the teacher. If I was calm and deliberate, I projected a calming effect on the class.

CHOOSING WHO TO BECOME

Teachers like Richard and Hank provided a welcome contrast to Ron Johnson and Mr. Costello. Though unaware at the time, I was starting to choose who to become, a process that was more visceral than intellectual. I felt myself drawn to certain teachers, teachers whose actions implied a vision of human capacity that resonated with some essential beliefs I held but could not articulate. I liked Richard and Hank. I was starting to dislike Ron and Mr. Costello. I also discovered I was not especially fond of Barbara Madison.

In 1982, Barbara Madison was a nationally recognized educator who wrote books and led workshops. She was famous for a "model" of teaching that was easy to learn. I say model because its features were primarily technical. There were steps. You followed them. There were reasons for the steps, but the model was mainly about the steps, not the reasons.

Dr. Madison—she was a professor on the west coast—would be coming to our district for an "in-service" day. This was a big deal. For a small, out of the way school district in upstate New York to score such a well-known presenter was very unusual. She must have been expensive because our superintendent arranged with the neighboring superintendent to bring all the teachers from both districts to our high school auditorium for a three-hour session.

Barbara Madison arrived in a limousine. I know this because as I arrived—in my Nissan Sentra—I saw her car parked near the back door of the auditorium. The auditorium was full, with 500 teachers all on their contractually arranged day away from the classroom set aside for the purpose of in-service learning. Barbara Madison was down front, instructing from an overhead projector.

A very big screen at the front of the auditorium displayed elements of her model, featuring her hands in motion with a pen underlining key points and adding notes. Dr. Madison spoke vigorously, excitedly, and she seemed a bit discombobulated. She glanced from side to side. She consulted notes. She paused repeatedly. Her timing was off. It was as though she had forgotten she was doing this presentation until the last minute and was faking her way through a smooth delivery. There was sufficient muscle memory that she could still get a chuckle from the crowd and cleverly win over the room.

Then she began swinging her arms around her ears and hair, swatting at a fly. Finally, the fly came to rest on the projecting surface. Everyone saw it enlarged many, many times on the screen. Dr. Madison did not catch on that the fly showed up on the screen, but everybody saw it clear as day.

She kept on with her presentation. She was showing us the steps of a sample lesson. Everyone in the room, however, was watching closely to see how this great teacher of teachers would respond to a simple classroom challenge. Would she lose her composure? Would she be cool, make a joke, and move on? Would the fly persist and undo her? Would she swat it and squash it on the projection surface?

She pressed on with the sample lesson, now at step five. Swat. Now step six. Swat, swat. This group of 500 teachers, each of whom had been just barely willing to give the limo-chauffeured expert a chance, was beginning to turn. How would a person unable to manage a simple teaching challenge deal with a room full of eighth graders? She whacked the side of the machine, missed, and pressed on to step nine. Still, she did not acknowledge the fly to her audience. At some point, the fly decided to leave poor Dr. Madison alone, but it was too late. The fly had been a test, and, in the eyes of her audience, the expert had failed.

Next day, Hank and Roy were at their end of the table in the teacher's lounge. Encircled in the usual cloud of smoke, they swatted and speechified. When the bell rang, they snuffed out their cigarettes and headed off to class to teach as they were accustomed. Just before he slipped into the hallway, Hank turned and gave me a wink. I was sitting on the vinyl upholstered couch near the door. It was a wink that said, We both know what's up.

I was flattered that Hank thought I was in on the secret, whatever the secret was. It was a wink that made me feel a little pulse of well-being. I tried to sort out why, as I sat there staring at the ninth grade social studies textbook. It was gray and blandly title *Exploring Asia and Africa.* Teachers were moving in and out of the faculty room with the change of periods. For me, my prep period had just ended and my lunch period was about to begin, which is why I could sit there through the hubbub. Ron Johnson bustled by and slapped me on the knee.

"Look lively, Nehring. The day won't wait." He brushed past me and headed for the ditto machine without looking back. I realized all of a sudden that I'd been hoping Dr. Madison would point the way for me. I'd been hoping that whatever the famous intellectual from the big university said or did would settle everything in me that was unsettled about what it means to be a teacher.

I watched Ron carefully place his ditto master on the cylinder of the ditto machine and started to crank, slowly at first, making sure the master adhered smoothly to the drum. But the famous intellectual, with her steps and her scripted routines, was completely underwhelming. I was going to have to figure things out for myself. So I thought about Ron Johnson and Mr. Costello and all the other teachers who bought into the boot camp approach to middle school teaching. It was more than an approach, I realized. It was the outward expression of a vision for human capacity that was dark and fearful.

Dr. Madison, on the other hand, offered something that, though not dark, was just kind of flat and reductive. If the boot camp view of things said kids are like dogs, then Dr. Madison's view said kids are like robots. But kids are not like dogs. And they're not like robots. They're like me. They're curious, and they actually want to learn, given the right situation. They are capable of compassion and generosity, and they are capable of being insensitive and mean.

They have personalities. They enter my classroom with lives attached. They are complicated. So teaching—*good* teaching—has to be complicated, too. Believing that kids are like dogs or robots can be shortcuts that make life simple for the teacher. And when you're teaching upwards of 150 students, simple can be appealing. Was it possible to not give in to shortcuts? Could I do better? That wink from Hank, I decided, was an answer to my unspoken question. It said, yes, you can do better.

CHAPTER 3: REFLECTION QUESTIONS

1. What do you do with a student who is consistently angry or defiant?
2. How do you see students as individuals when they come at you in groups of twenty or thirty, six times a day?
3. Does good teaching require you to see your students as individuals? Do you have to know a student well in order to teach him or her well?
4. What are the compromises teachers make to manage students in large numbers? What gets lost? Are some compromises better than others?
5. "Kids are like dogs" and "kids are like robots" are clearly poor ways to think about students. How *should* a teacher think about his or her students?
6. What does it mean for a principal to "support" his or her teachers? What should a principal do if the teacher has made a poor choice in responding to a classroom management issue?
7. What should a teacher say or do after recognizing he or she has made a misstep in managing a student-related issue?
8. How do you find your competence and your compass when you are overwhelmed by a new job?
9. Are there people in places you've worked whom you admire? Are there people whose work you do not respect? What are their qualities? How have they influenced you?
10. Does the way you see your students reflect the way you see people in general? Should it?
11. Have you ever lost your way professionally and then found it? What happened? Was there a turning point, or, perhaps, more than one? What can you learn from the experience?

SUGGESTED READING

The seminal work about the culture of teaching in American schools is Dan Lortie's *Schoolteacher: A Sociological Study*. For a gritty account of a day at school from the perspective of a teacher, consider, *Why Do We Gotta Do this Stuff, Mr. Nehring? Notes from a Teacher's Day in School*, by James Nehring. By far, the best book on shortcuts that are forced on teachers by the system is Theodore Sizer's *Horace's Compromise: The Dilemma of the American High School*.

FOUR

TEACHING AND COACHING

That spring, the principal said to me, "The high school needs an assistant track coach," and I thought I could take on the role. I was a recreational runner. Here's the thing about track: how good you are is visible to all. By the end of the first day, everyone knows that Kevin is the fastest runner, Josh, Jacob, and Peter are the slowest runners, and there's a large middle of the pack where everyone else runs. Everybody accepts this. Everyone strives for everyone else to get better. It's just the way school might be in a dream.

I ran with the team every day. I didn't follow behind in a golf cart barking peppy commentary, the way I saw other coaches do. Kevin was faster than me. I was faster than Josh, Jacob, and Peter. I ran somewhere in the large middle. Everyone accepted this, too, including Kevin, who still listened to me even though he was a much better athlete.

I enjoyed great freedom to coach as I wished. There was no curriculum to follow. So track became an extension of what I brought to it. I played endlessly with inventive ideas. Since I was in charge of the long distance runners, our afternoons were spent mostly on the country roads surrounding the high school. Early in my coaching, the veteran runners showed me the routes. As time went by, I found new ones. One weekend, I made a dozen photocopies of a map that showed the roads around the school. I outlined a different route on each one, wrote the mileage, and named it after a runner: Evan's Errand, Roger's Ramble. I laminated the maps and put them in a notebook that we had at practice each day. Some team members came up with new routes and new names. We put them in the book.

Instruction was done on the run.

Me: Hey, Tim.

Tim: Hey. (Puff puff.)

Me: I've noticed something.

Tim: What's that?

Me: When you run, your arms are scrunched up like this. (I demonstrate with my arms tucked into my chest.) I want them more at your side. Elbows 90 degrees. Like a pendulum, they rock you forward. (I demonstrate. Tim glances at me.)

Tim: Okay.

Me: Do it.

Tim: (Moves his arms off his chest.)

Me: More. Open up your elbows. 90 degrees. (Tim follows my instructions.)

Me: Good.

Sometimes, the answer wasn't so clear, and instruction was more of a joint diagnosis.

Me: (Running hard to keep up with Kevin. Puff puff.) Kevin.

Kevin: Hi.

Me: You had a lot left at the end of your mile yesterday.

Kevin: What do you mean?

Me: (Puff puff.) You had a big kick, lasted almost (puff puff) the whole last quarter.

Kevin: Uh huh.

Me: You think you saved too much for the end?

Kevin: Umm. Maybe.

Me: Your last split was twenty seconds faster than the first three.

Kevin: Huh?

Me: I think (puff puff) go out faster maybe, just a bit.

Kevin: I can try. Like an experiment.

Me: (Puff puff). Like an experiment. I'll time your splits.

I often think about the benefits of applying the concepts of coaching in the classroom: there are team goals and individual goals; there's no shame in whatever performance level you occupy, and if there were, you'd have to deal with it because it is public every day; and there's recognition that some things come easy to a few individuals and others have to work hard for it.

There's respect for those who work hard, regardless of achievement. There's high praise for those who improve, there's awe for those who achieve absolutely, and there's disapproval for those with huge natural talent who fail to work hard. There's deep admiration for those who work hard with less natural ability. Those who come in with prior experience and training are encouraged to share it with the rest. Their development is understood, at least in part, as a product of their experience and training.

Imagine if the privileged kids arriving in kindergarten from homes with educated parents and years of nurturing pre-school were encouraged to share with the rest and if their skill level was openly recognized as the result of some prior experience and training. Imagine if there were shared admiration for those who worked hard and achieved on a relative scale while those who had much naturally (or from experience and training) and failed to work hard, faced disapproval.

Coaching track reminded me daily that my students are individuals. Dr. Madison somehow missed this, and the Ron Johnsons of the world denied it entirely. But it was undeniable. It began to seep into my teaching. I wanted to know my students better, and they showed an interest in me. They started to show up after school for various reasons, beginning around December.

TWO BOYS

On the last day of school before Christmas, Nathan and Felix appeared in my classroom at the end of the day. Nathan was short with a mouthful of braces, and at fourteen, still more boy than man. Felix was tall, lean, and quiet, a counterpoint in physique and affect to his talkative friend. Felix looked to Nathan to speak.

"Hey, Mr. Nehring," said Nathan.

"Hi, Nathan. Hi, Felix."

"Hey, so we got you a Christmas present." They both chuckled. I wondered if this was some kind of joke. I decided to act like it was for real, in case it was.

Nathan looked at Felix and Felix reached into his pocket and pulled out an item the size of a pack of cigarettes. It was covered in yellow wrapping paper with small blue birthday cakes. He placed it on the corner of my desk.

"How nice of you guys. You didn't have to do this." They both giggled. "Should I open it?"

"That's generally what you do, Mr. Nehring." Nathan said this, and as with much of what Nathan said, I wondered if it was cheekiness or just boyish cluelessness about tone. I let it go.

"Okay." I made a show of unwrapping it, pulling the tape free to avoid tearing the paper to slow down the process and make it special for two boys bringing a present to their teacher. It was a bottle of men's cologne, an Avon product, sample size. I made big, like it was a grand gift. Both boys giggled again and shifted. I decided it was not a trick of any kind. They were acting far too awkward for a gag.

"Cool!" I offered. I unscrewed the top, smelled the bottle, pursed my lips with approval, looked at the boys, nodded, and said, "Nice." With a bit of flourish, I upended the bottle and daubed some cologne in my palm, put down the bottle, patted my two palms together, then patted my cheeks, just like in a commercial.

"Okay, there we go." I said. "Cologne! Thank you, Felix. Thank you, Nathan. That's really thoughtful of you. I like it a lot."

The two boys continued to shift, looking everywhere but at me—at their feet, at each other, at the clock.

"Well, I guess we better go," said Nathan.

"Yeah," said Felix.

"Okay, well thanks again, boys. This was really nice of you."

"All right. See ya," said Nathan.

They both turned and headed for the door. Just before they left the room, Felix turned, and, gaining his courage at the very last moment, called, "Bye, Mr. Nehring," and waved.

"Bye, Felix."

Teaching Nathan and Felix after this episode was completely different. Our small, shared experience, their gesture of affection, and my appreciation for their gift built trust, a bond that had huge payoff in the classroom. The boys started to do their homework because they did not want to disappoint a teacher they liked. And I changed, too. I wanted them to succeed because I cared about them. I liked them.

Little things changed in my teaching after that. I made more eye contact. I noticed them—when they were or were not paying attention, when it looked like they got whatever we were talking about. I'd walk by their desk and ask a question when it looked like they were starting to drift. I smiled when they showed interest.

THREE GIRLS

Felicia, Alexandra, and Rose traveled as a threesome. I don't think they always traveled that way. I think it was just when they were on a mission involving me, since they were all three in the same class together, and since they were possibly afraid to approach me singly. Felicia had been out sick for two days, and on day three she was apparently well enough to come after school and make the rounds to each teacher to inquire about the work she'd missed.

The three enter my room with Alexandra in the lead. Alexandra, who is serious and sophisticated like her name, has the bearing of a journalist. No fear. She would come alone if she needed to, but she is here for her friend.

"Hi, Mr. Nehring," Alexandra says from the doorway where the three of them stand. "Do you have a minute?" What fourteen year-old says *do you have a minute*?

"Of course," I answer.

They enter, Alexandra still leading. I watch them as they cross the space between the door and my desk, Felicia and Rose speeding up to match Alexandra's confident stride. They arrive at my desk. Alexandra turns to Felicia to prompt her.

"Gee, how are *you* feeling?" I ask before Felicia speaks.

This somehow confuses the script that Felicia has in her head. She is bright but shy. Her presence is tentative, like the fairies that decorate the margins of old-fashioned children's books. A moderate wind could blow her away. She speaks almost in a whisper, and not because she is getting over being sick.

"Oh, I'm okay. Thanks. I came to get my homework."

"You brought your support team with you." I nod toward her friends.

"Oh," she offers, as if surprised to discover that she has two friends at her side.

"Oh," she says again, this time with a lift, a suggestion of laughter, like she is acknowledging my joke, thinking perhaps, belatedly, she is *expected* to acknowledge my joke, and wishes to be polite. Felicia turns her head toward Alexandra and then toward Rose, both of whom remain silent.

Felicia speaks. "I was wondering if I could have the work I missed."

"Absolutely, I'm glad you stopped by."

I shift into business mode, explaining what we did in class and concluding with a neat list of to-dos that will get her caught up with the rest of the class. But even as I say, "you'll be all caught up," I know it's not completely true. One can't really make up the classroom experiences one has missed: the discussions, the small group exercises, the spontaneous events that slowly build thinking skills and habits of mind. One has to be there to benefit from it.

"Oh, thank you, Mr. Nehring," says Felicia as though I've just given her a cup of water in the desert.

"You're welcome, Felicia."

"Well, bye," she says.

They all nod and turn to leave. Then they're out the door.

I wish Ron Johnson had been right there beside me. I would have turned to him and asked, 'Kids are like dogs? Really?' I wondered about Dr. Madison. I knew there wasn't a word in her vocabulary for any of this. There were no steps involved. No script. But Hank would get it. He understood students were complicated, like himself, like me, like everyone.

Still, there was a hard truth to be learned. Most of the time, I saw my students in large groups, and I had to design lessons for those groups. It wasn't all spontaneous, individual after-school encounters. And as much as I liked the ideas of athletic coaching as a way of teaching, I had limited time to make things happen.

Each day brought six waves of students through my door, and I had to shape something meaningful in the very precise forty-three minutes that they were delivered to me before the tide swept them back out the door and on to the next class. Somehow, I had to strike a balance between appreciating my students as individuals, managing them in large numbers, and teaching them something valuable.

TEACHING GANDHI

It was spring, and I was going to teach about Mohandas Gandhi. I was delighted that the New York State ninth grade curriculum included him, especially since it had recently come to light that a former school board member for the Middle Valley Schools also served in a somewhat less public capacity as Grand Wizard of the Ku Klux Klan. Middle Valley was not known for its progressive values.

I loved the story of Gandhi and his successful non-violent campaigns that produced such an extraordinary result—independence for the subcontinent. There was his early failure as an attorney in India, his experiments in South Africa with non-violence, his return to India, his travels by train across his country, the evolution of his political strategies, the drama of mass events like the Dandi Salt March and Gandhi's numerous hunger strikes, his brilliant negotiations with colonial officials, and, the irony of the outcome—an independent but divided land.

The more I learned about Gandhi, the more I wanted to tell other people about him. Since my students were a captive audience, I could easily spend a day or two telling them about Gandhi. I could dramatize the Dandi Salt March—how Gandhi set out from his ashram with a handful of friends and walked nearly three hundred miles, speaking and gathering followers as he went, and how there were nearly 30,000 when he arrived at the shore of the Indian Ocean; how, standing on the beach, he reached down to pick up the muddy sand, held it aloft and declared that the salt it contained is every Indian's birthright. It would be fun and easy, but it would be telling, not teaching.

What would my students be doing? They would probably be listening because everybody likes a good story. But what would they make of it? What did I *want* them to make of it? I couldn't just tell the story without there being a reason for telling the story. What did I want my students to learn? What were my objectives? Anabel McCourt and Alistair Hollingberry had become my inner voice. I decided that coming out the other side of such a lecture, I would want my students to be able to recount the story themselves with an understanding of the key events and, moreover, I wanted my students to ask themselves, "In what ways did Gandhi succeed? Why? In what ways did he fail? Why?"

These were questions with multiple answers. What could I do as the teacher to increase the odds that my students would, in fact, do these things, as opposed to simply listening—or not—to a pretty good teacher story?

I decided to begin the lesson by asking my students to imagine that they were in a school where all the teachers were mean and gave way too much homework. I told them to imagine that everybody knew about the situation, and all the students were angry about it, but nobody knew what to do. With that, pretty much the whole class sat up. Can you think, I asked them, of some action you might take that could actually result in a positive change?

"What if I just refuse to do homework?" said Jared, addressing his classmates from his seat near the back of the room.

There was an edge of defiance in his voice, and I liked the direction of Jared's comment, so I pressed him.

"Then you'd just get an even lower grade."

"But what if none of us did the homework," Melissa added. "If nobody did homework, then what would they do, fail us all?" Melissa clearly had a future as a labor organizer.

"I think we would work really hard," said Kristina from the other side of the room. "We would show our teachers that we're really smart, and we would work hard and then they wouldn't be mean."

After several minutes of talk, the class was fired up about what to do. Then I explained about the Indian people being under British colonial rule and how the Indians were angry about it, but nobody knew what to do. Then, I said, I was going to tell them the story of a person who figured out what to do and it worked. Everybody was with me. Even Todd Harper, who seemed stuck between wanting to do something subversive and wanting to hear me out. He looked around the room, saw everyone was caught up in the lesson, and decided to sit still. Then he looked at me, actually looked up and met my gaze with a kind of passive stare, slack-jawed.

I asked everyone to listen carefully to my lecture and then, when it was over, to write down three things from the lecture that seemed especially important to Gandhi's success. When the lecture was finished, I had the class move into small groups to combine lists, come up with an outline for the lecture, and write their outline on the chalkboard.

They compared the outlines and debated what was better about one or the other. I thought about a March day, just two years before, when I visited Mr. Conklin's class and how I worried that indoor work meant a compromise. I could move out of the cold, but I'd have to torture adolescents with boring work. I looked around the classroom, *my* classroom. Kids were out of their chairs—even Todd Harper—talking about Gandhi without me forcing them to engage. I was teaching not telling, the way Alistair Hollingberry had wanted. I was using Annabel McCart's lesson design for active learning. Ken would have liked it, Hank would approve.

NEW JEOPARDY

Sometimes it feels as though every social studies teacher in America plays *Jeopardy* every Thursday to get students ready for the test on Friday. Suppose tomorrow's test is on World War I. The *Jeopardy* categories will be: long term causes, immediate causes, allies and enemies, famous battles, Treaty of Versailles.

"Mr. Jones, I'll take 'Treaty of Versailles' for fifty, please," a student might say.

Just like the TV show, students pick categories and dollar amounts and answer questions, or, in the true spirit of the game, provide a question to go with the answer.

It's clever and hip and fast-paced and focuses students on course content. I noticed other teachers using it. Their classrooms were boisterous. I'd walk by and it sounded like a pep rally. My students said, "Hey Mr. Nehring, can we play *Jeopardy*? We used to play it in Mrs. Anderson's class."

So I played it. I prepared forty "answers" in advance that could be completed with "Who is ..." or "What is ..." questions. And there was plenty of enthusiasm and cheering and clapping and competitive angst. It was, indeed, like a pep rally. It also involved about as much brain power as a pep rally. Easy items, the ones that got you $20 on the game board, were factual in nature.

"This European nation, bordering Germany, saw some of the bloodiest battles of the war."

"What is France?"

Items that got you $100 on the game board were harder, but only because they were more obscure.

"This French king was famous for extravagant parties at the location where the treaty concluding World War I was later held."

"Who is Louis the XIV?"

The game lacked real challenge. It also lacked involvement. Despite all the cheering and hoopla, at any given moment, there was only one student in the classroom who had to think—the student trying to remember the less obscure or more obscure fact for game dollars. Everyone else in the room was off the hook.

This was a problem. I couldn't *not* do the game since, having once played it, I was now expected to offer it regularly as the pre-test review strategy of choice. I would be the completely uncool teacher if I just stopped. On the other hand, if I aspired to teach something more than dates, famous people, and famous events, I had to somehow up the ante.

So I created *New and Improved Jeopardy*. It was May. Track season was in full swing. Windows and doors were open during the day. You could hear voices of younger kids outside at recess. I could occasionally hear Hank across the hall. There were birds in the trees and occasional warm breezes. It was hard to pay attention. The situation called for drastic measures.

For homework, I told everyone to bring all their notes and books to class the next day.

"But Mr. Nehring, it's still like, three days before the test."

"Right," I said.

The next day, everyone showed up with all their stuff.

"Okay, so we're making five groups of five. Count off." I point to different places in the classroom and tell the groups to circle up. "Bring all your stuff with you," I add. Chairs scrape across the linoleum and oversized backpacks go *thwump* as students drop them on the floor. After sixty seconds of chaos, students are more or less settled in their groups. Some are even looking over at me waiting for instructions.

"Okay," I begin. "This is *New Jeopardy*." This is met with groans. Anything described as "new" must mean more work, less fun. "Somebody picks a category and then I give a question to the whole class. Then, I'll give you thirty seconds with your group to come up with an answer. You can use your notes and your books and talk to everyone in your group. Once you have an answer, make sure everyone in your group is ready to say it. After a while, I'll call time, which means everyone has to stop talking. Then, I'll roll a die and that will decide which group gives the answer. I will then call on a particular member of that group to speak for the group. At that point, no one can say anything. That person will give the answer for the group while the whole class is silent. Then I will point to one member of each of the other teams and ask, 'Do you agree or disagree?' Once each team has spoken, I will announce if the answer that the first group gave is correct or incorrect. If the answer was correct, you get the points. Then, if your group agreed with the correct answer, you get points too. If your group disagreed with the correct answer, then you don't get points. Reverse is true too."

I look at the class. They're looking back. I can't tell if they're with me or just kind of stunned.

"What happened to the money?" Mike asks.

"Mike, the truth is, there never was any money, but there's still points and there's still some friendly competition."

"Why the books? We can like just read the answer." This is tiny Helene, a spitfire of a kid who is never intimidated by bigger people, which, in her case, is almost everyone.

"I *want* you to read the answer," I say in a cool tone. "I want you to *find* the answer, and I want you to take good notes every day and keep your stuff organized so that whenever we play *New Jeopardy* you can find the answer."

I scan the class and see that the signal is coming across for those who are tuned in.

"Can't we just raise our hand if we know the answer?" Helene asks again.

"No."

"Why not?"

"Because I want you to share the answer. I want you to work togeth-er."

"But isn't that cheating?"

"It's not a test. It's a review for a test."

New Jeopardy worked. My students wanted it because it was still, more or less, *Jeopardy*—what all the cool teachers did. And while they consid-ered *New Jeopardy* weird, they knew I was in love with my creation and wasn't going to back down. For me, *New Jeopardy* was a turning point. With it, I took a stand against the drift of the culture I had entered. It was something I could proudly tell Hollingberry, McCart, and Ken about. But it was also something that Ron Johnson and Mr. Costello recognized as normal.

If either of them walked by my classroom and heard someone shout, "What was . . . the treaty of Versailles?" They would think, Nehring's finally getting the hang of it. Little did they know I had found a way to fly under the radar of a culture that was part boot camp, part pep rally. Like the adolescents I taught, I was engaged in a process of individua-tion, and I was beginning to understand who I might become as a teacher and what school might become, given the opportunity for something different.

CHAPTER 4: REFLECTION QUESTIONS

1. Should teaching be more like athletic coaching? What would change?
2. What changes about teaching when a student and a teacher build a relationship? Does it make for better learning?
3. Why is lecturing a limited teaching strategy? Why do many teach-ers continue to use it? How can a lecture be modified to make it a better teaching strategy?
4. Sometimes students are excited and engaged without learning much. What's missing? How can you keep the excitement and up the intellectual demand?

SUGGESTED READING

For a powerful meditation on the centrality of relationships to teaching, read Parker Palmer's, *The Courage to Teach: Exploring the Inner Landscape of a Teacher's Life*. For a book on great strategies to build student engage-ment, read *Strategies that Promote Student Engagement: Unleashing the De-*

sire to Learn by Ernestine Riggs and Cheryl Gholar. By rooting the work in a thoughtful understanding of learning psychology, the authors make the power of effective teaching strategies both clear and persuasive.

FIVE

A PLEASANT ROUTINE

My wife Laurie and I met in Middle Valley in September during our first year teaching at a tea for new teachers hosted by the Board of Education. Two years later, we got married. A year after that, we moved upstate to Albany. Laurie left teaching and went to graduate school while I worked in one district and then another where the money was better. We bought a house in a neighborhood known quaintly as Old Delmar, in the town where I taught. I also bought an old fashioned-leather briefcase, and Laurie got me a three-speed bike for my ride to work.

School fell into a pleasant routine. I rode my bike to and from work, taught my five classes, enjoyed the camaraderie of the faculty room, designed lessons, and read student work. Laurie took to calling me Mr. Rogers. She bought me a cardigan sweater. We took walks after dinner and sat on the porch swing and waved to neighbors as they passed on their evening walks. I took on advising the student newspaper and the Model United Nations.

HOW DO YOU ASK A QUESTION?

For several years, I coached a Model United Nations Team composed almost entirely of boys who were keen on showing off their vast knowledge of international affairs, their acumen for gamesmanship, and their ability to argue a point—not unlike most legislative bodies. Model UN met in my classroom every Wednesday afternoon. Our weekly meetings were supposed to be training sessions for the Model UN conferences that we attended a couple times during the year along with thirty or forty other schools.

Each team was assigned a nation and there would ensue a grand simulation with a General Assembly, Security Council, proposals, and usually a crisis, inserted by the teachers part-way into the conference proceedings. During our weekly club meetings we were supposed to be designing our proposal and conducting research, but my know-it-all boys had little interest in research. Their interest was in showing each other how much they already knew.

Our meetings tended to go like this: ten minutes after the last bell rings, no one has showed up. I begin to feel like maybe I have reclaimed an hour in my day. Then Rajiv strides into the room.

"Where is everybody?"

I answer, "Spread across several continents, mostly in Asia." My standard line, and Rajiv shows no interest in it. He leaves the room, on a quest to round up his club-mates. If there are at least three or four of them, they can yammer at each other for an hour.

Next, Chip arrives. "Are we having Model UN today?"

I answer, "If enough people show up, we will."

"Hang on," says Chip and darts out of the room.

A minute later, Jake appears. "Anyone else here?"

I look up from my desk, "Well, Rajiv and Chip have been in and out. They're looking for you and your ilk."

"Huh." Jake exits.

Rajiv returns with Matt. "Okay, we're here. Anyone else show up?"

Looks like we will have Model UN after all. I start to wonder if I'll play a strong role or let the boy-energy play itself out without intervention.

Fifteen minutes later, all four boys are deep into a debate over Afghanistan, playing the United States (Chip), the Afghan government (Rajiv), the Mujahedeen rebel leaders (Matt), and Saudi Arabia (Jake). This was during the period of the Soviet intervention in Afghanistan.

"The Mujahadeen are freedom fighters," says Chip, playing the United States. He is pacing near Rajiv, who is seated playing the Afghan government.

Rajiv replies, "You dare to refer to these butchers, these terrorists, these rapists and murderers as freedom fighters? They are the most common, the lowest of thugs."

"Hah," says Jake, playing Saudi Arabia, "The simple matter is that your government is a puppet of the Soviet Union and Afghanistan is a powerless client state in a Soviet grab for dominance over the oil fields of the Middle East and control of the Black Sea."

Chip (United States) steps in again. "Yes, the Soviet Union cannot be allowed to unilaterally determine the fate of a geopolitically significant region. With their 1979 invasion, they clearly and flagrantly violated the sovereignty of the Afghan borders . . ."

"Rubbish!" Rajiv jumps in. "The sovereign government of Afghanistan was pleased to invite our friends, the Soviet Union to provide humanitarian and police support for our revolutionary agenda. I will re-

mind everyone that under my administration, there has been considerable progress made with land reform, women's rights, and education.

"And at what cost!" Matt, silent until now, playing a tribal chief with
the Mujahadeen, continues, "You have stripped us of our religion by
outlawing Islam. You have stripped us of our traditions by granting
women your so-called "rights," and you have stripped us of our property
with your despicable communist land grabs!"

"Here here!" cries the United States.

"Hold on just a minute," says Afghanistan.

"Allah be praised," says Saudi Arabia.

I liked my Model UN kids. They had passion, and they desperately
wanted to be experts. They loved using words that sounded smart, but
they were less committed to the work they needed to do to become truly
informed, and I was wondering whether the way we taught school was
letting them down. We weren't teaching them how to ask questions. This
got me wondering.

I was teaching the global studies curriculum at the time and could do
it blindfolded—which is never a good sign. I was itching to try something
new, and all the boy energy in Model UN had gotten me thinking. Students were expected, as per departmental guidelines, to write a research
paper sometime during the year. There was no written guide.

Instead, there was a powerful, unwritten set of norms that went something like this:

1. Students will be afraid of the research paper;
2. The research paper will feel to the student like climbing Mt. Everest;
3. The most important part of the research paper will be adherence to
   lots of rules about formatting, including margin width and precise
   rendering of citations;
4. After completing the research paper, the student will dread the
   thought of doing another one in tenth grade;
5. All of this will be construed as "academic rigor."

It was around this time that I learned about the "I-Search" paper, a different approach to research developed by an educator named Ken MacRorie. As so often happens in teaching, the "I-search" came to me not from
the source, but by derivative means, adapted and reshaped by inventive
colleagues, most of whom were in the English department, where student voice was valued.

At the time, I had no clue about Ken McRorie, but I sure liked his
approach to research. The "I-Search" paper is a process that asks the
student to identify something he or she truly wonders about, to frame it
as a question, to then look for answers to the question, documenting her
search process along the way. The final paper is a narrative of the process
of question formation and searching for an answer, followed by an expo-

sition of what was found in the search. The final part of an I-Search paper is the formation of a tentative thesis based on what was found. Imagine: the thesis comes at the end, not the beginning. The I-Search paper represents in narrative form the way a person thinks when they are using their mind well.

Once I heard about the I-Search paper, I had to try it out. I knew I was being subversive. My colleagues in the social studies department would not like this. So I modified the process slightly. The student had to identify a question that was in some way connected to what we were studying. They could *not* write about sports photography. They *could* write about early sailing ships.

What I did not anticipate—but should have—was the resistance from some of my students. Rajiv of the Model UN, for instance:

Rajiv: You want me to do what?

Me: I want you to tell me something you wonder about in connection with our studies.

Rajiv: I don't wonder about anything.

Me: Is there something you don't know that you'd like to know?

Rajiv: That's your job. You teach us stuff so we'll know it.

Me: Right.

Rajiv: This isn't what a research paper is. A research paper is when you give us topics, we pick one, we research it, and we write a paper with a thesis that we back up with evidence.

Me: Well, that's one kind of research paper. There is another kind, which you are going to do in this class, where you tell the story of your thesis and how you got there.

Rajiv: We're writing stories? I thought this was social studies. This sounds baby-ish.

I got a similar reception from my colleagues in the social studies department.

"The I-Search is a research paper with training wheels," said Fran, our supervisor, during a department meeting. He intended this remark supportively, since my students were ninth graders.

"It's a stepping stone for ninth graders," said Ray, sounding diplomatic. Ray taught Advanced Placement U.S. history.

The Social Studies department was the land of *tough*, the land of *rigor* and *content*, where conversation often turned to lamentations of our school's decline from a golden era when students came to school with bright faces, eager to do hard work. Lurking beneath these comments was a contempt for anything progressive sounding. The I-Search was in their crosshairs.

Meanwhile, Rajiv, Jake, and Chip of Model UN were reconciling themselves to their strange assignment. I coaxed them with the suggestion that they think about their I-Search project as data gathering for a Model UN conference.

Rajiv wondered if the Mujahadeen were a unified movement or an alliance of convenience assembled to oppose the Soviets. Still, he resisted inserting himself into his narrative. His writing was telegraphic: "searched library shelves in 900s for biography, turned up nothing. Borrowed friend's copy of Encyclopedia of Middle East, read about nation formation in Afghanistan." He literally left the pronoun "I" out of his I-Search.

He refused to identify himself as a person who did not know something. Such an admission would, from his perspective, make him appear weak and vulnerable, the wolf with the broken leg who would slow down the pack and have to be left behind to die.

School teaches students to advocate, to speak regardless of whether they have first listened. We teach our students to write a thesis paper, conduct a debate, give three reasons, and be persuasive. It's no wonder that by the time they get to a doctoral program—as I was to later discover—that they sometimes don't know how to ask a question. Good teaching is about good questions: finding them, asking them, pursuing them, being okay with not fully answering them, and then identifying the next question. But schools, at least the schools I had spent time in during the first five years of my teaching career, did not really value questions.

I was starting to see a deep institutional deficiency that extended beyond the classroom. As long as students didn't ask questions, we could batch process them in large groups, just like a factory. Once questions entered the picture, the assembly line slowed down. When different students asked different questions, then whole-class instruction started to break down entirely. The assembly line ground to a halt. So, you either had to discourage questions, or you had to re-think how you taught.

If you were going to embrace questions, then you had to be ready to shift from deliverer-of-information to coach. And if you were going to become the coach, then you necessarily had to get to know your students as individuals. This was an alien priority for schools.

My teachers in high school did not know me. They were friendly enough, and they were very capable as teachers, but to them, I was a student somewhere in the middle of the room. In tenth grade, I was struggling in trigonometry, odd because I was in the honors group. Mrs. Kariannis decided I just needed more time. So when there was a test, I got to go to a quiet room all by myself, and I got to take as much time as I wanted. This didn't help.

My problem was that the math was demanding that I think in a way that did not come naturally to me. I had to think sequentially, procedurally, methodically. My natural mode was intuitive, framing the big picture and then sketching in the details. Had Mrs. Kariannis understood that, she would have sat down with me and coached me through the thinking process required for math, but she did not know that, so she chalked up my problem to "math anxiety" and gave me more time, which ended up being more time to think intuitively, more time to do it the wrong way.

I had Mr. Wetherington for honors English where we read books I considered to be dreadfully boring at the time, like *Winesburg, Ohio* and *Miss Lonelyhearts*. I would try to read these books, but would start wandering half way through the second page. I wanted to read adventure stories: climbing Mount Everest, survival at sea in a life boat. This is what we read in sixth grade, but for some reason, after sixth grade, all the teachers must have agreed we should start reading boring books.

I wanted to say this to my English teachers. I imagined inviting them all to a meeting and showing them the books I really like and a bunch of other kids probably really like, too. But they were teachers after all and they knew stuff, and, apparently, one must stop reading the really interesting books somewhere around junior high school and enter the adult world of books you're supposed to read instead of the books you want to read.

Now that I was a teacher, I wondered to what degree I was failing to understand my students in the same way, like the boy who quietly showed up each day for third period and occupied a seat somewhere in the middle of the room and didn't say much, who dutifully turned in his homework and managed to slide in and out of the room more or less anonymously. Who was he? That student was actually most of the 100+ students I served. Did it have to be this way?

Truth was, my "Mr. Rogers' life" was starting to feel pretty boring. Everything was nice: nice commute, nice classes, nice briefcase. School felt routine. My students, whenever I got to know them, were not routine. School felt like it stood in the way of something better. Could school be re-arranged?

A LIFE RAFT APPEARS

"When you read a text, all you can really say about it is how you respond as you read it. For example, 'It moves along well here,' or 'It slows down here, and I get confused about where it's headed.'" Mary was talking energetically to our Thursday afternoon writers' group: four English teachers, a physics teacher, the school librarian, and me, a mostly social studies teacher.

We were all restless with school and we'd just sort of found each other. Our writers group was about more than writing. We were about fundamentally disturbing school as we knew it.

Mary continued, "A writer remains in charge of her work. Readers say how they experience her text. She revises as she chooses. The more readers she hears from, the more informed her revision process. The more experienced her readers, the more sophisticated her revision process."

Mary was describing an alternative approach to the teaching of writing that she had been experimenting with. It positioned the teacher not as the all-knowing dictator of what is right and wrong. Instead, the teacher is a writer with more experience, a writer whose opinion especially matters, but who, ultimately, can only speak from his or her experience, just like anybody else. Which meant that the student-as-writer remained in charge of his or her own work.

We were all seated together in Mary's classroom, which featured posters of famous writers. We were under the watchful eyes of Ernest Hemingway, Oscar Wilde, James Joyce with round rim glasses, Hunter S. Thompson, and others.

Mary continued her explanation while I thought about how this would go down in the social studies department, the land of "we know what students need and we are right." Mary was the core of our writers group, which met most Thursdays after school. We brought fragments: three pages of a short story, part of an essay, a character sketch, a piece of dialogue, even a whole poem. Writing brought us together, but that wasn't all. Our raft of desks was a lifeboat to which we swam weekly.

We shared a restlessness with school: its stark uniformity, its obsession with order, the absence of curiosity or any shared vision, its overall dysfunction as an organization held together by contracts and conventions, and the absence of any alternative, unless you were a family with money. Then there were alternatives, all kinds of alternatives, a wide range of private schools within fifteen miles, each with a distinct ethos and mission, a strong sense of community. But not here, where the floors were shiny and the desks were arranged neatly in columns and rows, and people charged through the day like herky-jerky, intersecting city traffic, governed by stoplights.

PRETTY MUCH IT

My life was in a groove. Thing is, if you ride a groove long enough, it becomes a rut. I'd head off on my bike in the early morning, birds singing in the new sun. I'd rumble-strip across the final stretch of sidewalk, lock up my bike and head inside to teach my five classes, cover my forty-five minutes of hall duty, eat lunch with an assortment of colleagues—some lively and curious, a few burnt out and badly in need of retirement.

Then I'd do whatever after-school obligation went with the day of the week—Tuesday after-school help, Wednesday Model UN, Thursday, writers group. Then I'd head home, reverse rumble strip, busier streets with kids and cars and school buses. Then there'd be an hour or two lull before meeting Laurie in the kitchen, getting dinner, taking a stroll together after dinner, reading some student work, and making sure I was ready for tomorrow's classes. That was pretty much it. Within a few short years, I had constructed a life in the model of the old-fashioned, down home, high school teacher. It offered stability, purpose, community, and standing. Not to mention a bike and leather briefcase. But there was another side to this traditional role. The flip side of the beloved, brief case toting, bicycle riding, front porch swinging icon was something entirely less appealing.

Around this time, if someone asked me at, say, a Christmas party for Laurie's company, "What do you do?" I'd say, "I'm a teacher." The conversation would then follow a fairly predictable path.

"Oh, what do you teach?"

"I teach social studies, and sometimes English." I learned to say 'and sometimes English' because I got tired of hearing, 'Oh, social studies. I hated social studies.'"

"Oh. Hmm. What grade do you teach?"

"Mostly ninth graders."

"Oh, ninth grade."

The "oh" here is stated with emphasis "oooohhhhh" suggesting that the person, who probably has not set foot in a ninth grade classroom since he or she was in ninth grade, knows everything about it.

"That's such a difficult age."

That was the remark I really grew to resent, partly because of all the "ages" I've taught, I have not found ninth grade to be more or less difficult than any other. And partly because it always carried a hint of "you poor bastard stuck in a crappy job."

To this standard remark, I developed responses that I would pull out when I felt like taking charge of the conversation, like, "Oh, really? What do you find difficult about it?" Or "Well, I find ninth graders less difficult than adults, actually."

In my dreams, here's how the conversation goes from there:

Party guest: "Oh, ninth grade. That's a difficult age."

Me: "Oh, really? What do you find difficult about it?"

Party guest: "Oh, well, you know, raging hormones, rebelliousness, and ob-no-xious!"

Me: "Huh, well, I find the most difficult age is adulthood. You know, adults bring so much baggage to class: divorce, aging parents, kids that they use as an excuse for not grading their homework, jobs, mid-life crisis, menopause, you name it, the list goes on."

I never really said this. I have a hard time being sarcastic in my non-dreaming life.

The message was being drummed into me that school teaching is generally not regarded as an intellectual line of work. I knew this going in, and I thought it would not bother me, and I learned, over time, that it did.

I thought it would be instantly clear to anyone I met that I was different, but it wasn't. Did I hand out endless worksheets? Was I a petty scold? Was I uninterested in ideas? Was I uninterested in my students? I wanted to say, "I'm not that kind of teacher. Really." It upset me at a deeper level, too. Because of the system which teaching finds itself part of—100+ students, five classes a day, factory-like conditions—it was hard for the work to be about ideas and relationships.

It was nearly impossible to practice teaching in a way that was intellectually defensible. There was huge pressure for the work to be about order and efficiency. Perhaps, the only relief for all that pressure was to have something else to do on the side that was about ideas and relationships.

Once, somebody said, "What do you do?"

I replied, "I'm a teacher."

The person continued, "Do you do anything else?"

I said, "No, I'm just a teacher."

Imagine:

What do you do? I'm a doctor. Do you do anything else? No, I'm just a doctor.

What do you do? I'm a software engineer. Do you do anything else? No, I'm just a software engineer.

The truth was, I *wanted* to do something else. Being just a teacher, in the system as we know it, was, after all, not sufficient. But I did not want to leave teaching. I wanted to change what it meant to be a teacher. I had arrived at the perfect situation: teaching and living in the same town, riding my bike along tree-lined streets to a school filled with well-nourished students ready to learn. But in the midst of my halcyon existence, I was restless.

CHAPTER 5: REFLECTION QUESTIONS

1. What role do questions play in good teaching?
2. This chapter suggests the way we organize school discourages questions. What do you think?
3. How does the system limit good teaching? In what ways can a teacher mitigate the limitations of the system? Is there a limit to what a teacher can do to overcome the system's limitations?
4. What exactly is *the system*? In what ways are the system and the individual teacher one and the same?
5. Who's in charge of a student's writing, the student or the teacher? In other words, how does a teacher manage the tension between her role as instructor and evaluator of writing and the student's agency/voice? What does good writing instruction look like when it is appropriately balancing these competing and conflicting priorities?

6. Is it enough to be *just* a teacher? Does a creative outlet besides teaching make a teacher better, or is it compensation for uninteresting work?

SUGGESTED READING

To learn more about the I-Search paper, invented by Ken Macrorie, read his book, *The I-Search Paper: Revised Edition of Searching Writing*. More than a textbook, it offers a fundamentally different stance toward writing instruction from what is typically found in school classrooms. For more on an approach to writing instruction that honors the student's agency and voice, read Peter Elbow's *Writing without Teachers*.

SIX

MYSTERY AND RESULTS

A year later, Laurie and I purchased twenty-one bundles of cedar shingles, enough to cover the sides of our house. It would be my summer project, what I would do besides teaching. Like other property maintenance tasks—lawn mowing, painting—it yielded a tangible result. All such work offers a welcome counterpoint to teaching where progress is veiled and so much of learning remains a mystery.

A teacher friend, Pete, who was ten years older than I, came over to help me erect the scaffolding that would give Laurie and me easy access to the second story. Pete and several teacher buddies had a summertime home repair business that flourished. During July and August, they would shed their teacherly blue blazer, and tie on a tool belt. I wondered, as we fitted the interlocking tubes of the scaffolding, if I might start a summer business to complement my teaching.

Pete wasn't the only teacher friend who did this. Eric played banjo in a band, and, though they performed throughout the year, they shifted into high gear every summer, playing at festivals and coffeehouses, parties, and church socials. Mary was director at a summer camp for girls. Tina and her husband went home to her parents' apple farm every summer to help out. Harold had a landscaping business. Tom built stone walls. Trade work during the summer, it seemed, was just part of being a teacher.

I spent the better part of the summer shingling our house. There were days when I felt I led the perfect work life as I imagined myself teaching during the school year and doing house projects during the summer. It would be just the right balance of mysterious indoor teaching work and results-oriented outdoor work. Maybe the reason I craved something besides *just* teaching was that I respected its fundamentally mysterious nature.

A friend used to say the greatest mystery in any classroom is what anyone is learning. So shingling and painting and building stone walls provided an ideal counterpoint.

But it wasn't going to change the system.

PITCHING STORIES

Several years earlier, I'd written an essay about a teacher's typical day at school. Laurie said it was pretty good. So I browsed the magazine racks at the library to see where it might fit, and I sent it off to the *Atlantic Monthly*, the *American Scholar*, the *New Yorker* and several other magazines that appeared to publish longish, literary essays and stories.

There must be a thousand people around the country every day who do the same thing, utterly clueless about the volume of submissions these magazines receive, the super high quality of work they publish, and the long apprenticeship through which the vast majority of writers must labor before seeing their work published, if ever, in any of these magazines. But there is nothing to stop eager amateurs, full of hope, from running headlong into a brick wall.

All the magazines I listed rejected my essay. Thus began my apprenticeship as a writer, though I did not recognize it as such. All I knew at the time is that I wanted to write, and I wanted an audience for what I wrote. So I retrenched and started with a union newsletter that included updates from the executive committee and laudatory feature stories about individual teachers around the district whom I interviewed.

This was back at the Middle Valley Middle School, in the days just before desktop publishing. I typed a two column format on legal size paper and hand-made the headlines with black decals. Then, my sister-in-law gave me a copy of *The Writer's Handbook* for Christmas and I was introduced to the world of freelance writing. Here was a directory of magazines and book publishers, complete with contact information for pitching a story. It included an introductory chapter on the business of freelancing.

I wrote a travel article about the trip to Egypt that Laurie and I took for our honeymoon, including a five-day sailing adventure on the Nile in an open boat. I sent it off to *Cruising World* magazine with a set of color slides, and, lo and behold, several weeks later a contract appeared in the mail, and, several weeks after I returned the contract, a check for 600 dollars appeared.

Sadly, however, the article did not appear. It was never published. Next, I did a piece on a nearby apple orchard. I interviewed the man and woman who owned it and had run it for many years. I spent a morning with the migrant workers among the rows of trees. Again, I took color pictures. This time I got paid, *and* I got published.

Meanwhile, I kept teaching. What I really wanted to write about was my world in the classroom. Somewhere, I had read about the idea of writing a column for your local newspaper. So I put together three sample articles for an imagined column called, "In the Classroom." I sent them off to the editor of our town newspaper. A phone call and a lunch date with the editor got me the job. For two years, I wrote every other week about fictionalized students and teachers and school life.

I was reading writers' magazines now on trips to the library, and I started to notice ads for summer writing camps, most of which involved spending a week on a college campus with well-known writers who led workshops in short fiction, memoir, non-fiction, and so on. I signed up for the Wesleyan Writer's Workshop in Connecticut. It was affordable and nearby. Attending opened my eyes to bigger possibilities. I came home and decided to write a book.

This was pure hubris. Despite my failure several years before with an essay-length story of a teacher's day at school, I felt the tug of a book based on the same concept. It would have eight chapters, one for each period of the day. I had been reading James Herndon's books about teaching and loved his narrative style. I could do that. I decided I would write five pages per week for one full school year. I'd write the book front to back, starting with first period and plowing through the day. In a year, I'd have a completed manuscript. I already had the first two pages, composed as an exercise in my summer workshop.

I got to work. By November, I had the first two chapters and a prospectus. I sent the package off to several agents in New York and kept writing. The antidote for the anxiety of waiting to hear, I decided, was to keep writing. When rejections came in, the antidote for that was to send out more queries. Through the winter, the rejections and the manuscript pages piled up.

One agency wrote that the manuscript was unprofessionally written and no publisher in North America would want it. I almost stopped writing, except that writing had become automatic and so force of habit got me back to my desk on a regular basis to stick with my five-page quota each week. I'd write in the evening after doing the dishes, or I'd ask Laurie to do the dishes. "Sure, Jim," she'd say. "Go write your book."

Sometimes I'd write very early in the morning before any thoughts of the day got in the way. Or I'd have an idea at random moments, like reaching for a tomato with tongs at the salad bar in the cafeteria during lunch. I kept an index card in my shirt pocket for such moments, writing a quick note down before I forgot it. Immediate action became vital for harvesting ideas, phrases, and the right words. I found it useful to keep little writerly tips in mind when I wrote, such as, *don't be introspective, keep the writing on the action, use simple words,* and—my favorite—*don't be afraid to upset your mother,* which had been specifically invoked at my

Wesleyan summer camp by a workshop leader who had recently had his first book published, which later became a best seller.

This last tip was especially useful because I wanted to render hallway scenes true to life, which I could not do without introducing a good deal of salty language, which I knew would upset my mother. I decided two things about this book: first, I would do it and my mother would get over it; and second, if I was afraid of upsetting my mother, it meant I believed, at some level, that the book would be published.

I kept to five pages a week, and, in the middle of June, I finished chapter eight. Meanwhile, the rejections continued to pile up. Most were form letter rejections, and some of those were third or fourth generation photocopies, off center and barely legible. Once in a while, an editorial assistant would scrawl a short handwritten message in one corner: "Sorry, not for us." This, as unlikely as it might seem, gave me hope.

In idle moments, I would ponder the implications. *Not for us* could mean that it is for *somebody*, which means that it is good, but just not the sort of thing that this particular publisher wants right now. In more somber moments, I'd realize it was just a polite way of saying "not good enough" or maybe even "yuck" without having to actually say so.

One day in early August, a hand-addressed envelope arrived in the mail. The return address was an embossed imprint. It said M. Evans Publishers. I opened it. Inside was a piece of M. Evans embossed stationery with a hand-written note. It was cursive, tight little script that slanted downward across the page. "Dear Jim," it began. "You sent me several chapters of a book when I was at Dial Press, but I was not able to take action because we were not acquiring new manuscripts. I am now at M. Evans. If you haven't already sold the book, would you please send it to me? Thank you. Sincerely, Ferris Mack."

During the winter I had read a short notice, in the "Market Notes" section of a writing magazine that Ferris Mack at Dial Press was interested in non-fiction manuscripts. I had sent him my prospectus and sample chapters and had received a reply saying, "We are not acquiring new manuscripts at this time," which I took as just another variant of the polite rejection, especially since the ad had said this publisher *was* taking new manuscripts.

I quickly addressed a big envelope to Ferris Mack at M. Evans Publishers in New York City—I kept a couple prospectus-plus-manuscript packages in unaddressed envelopes ready to go—and flew on my bike to the post office to beat five o'clock. After that, time stood still for several weeks. I busied myself with cedar shingles and within a couple weeks, we finished the job. In late August, we went on vacation. When we got home, there was nothing in the mail from M. Evans Publishers.

Shortly, the school year started. I am always excited in the days just before school, and equally if not more excited as the year gets underway. I love meeting my new students. I find the uncertainty stimulating: Will I be able to work with these groups? Will we build a rapport? Will I remember how to teach? Maybe after eight years of teaching, I shouldn't have worried. But I worried, partly because I just did and partly because worry was a brace against over-confidence.

The affirmation I received from my students was the best antidote for the continual rejection I received from the publishing world. There were even times I completely forgot to wonder where my book might be—maybe at the bottom of the pile at the desk of some part-time editor in the basement or still sitting in the unsorted mail in a canvas bag with three hundred other manuscripts.

Besides teaching, I was starting classes in a doctoral program. If I could not get a book published, at least I could get another degree. I knew how to do that. So I applied and was admitted to the School of Education at SUNY Albany, and now, with the new school year, I was taking my first course.

All of this—the new school year and starting graduate school—served as excellent padding against the anticipated impact of another rejection. This one would be an especially severe blow since it had gotten me close and since, having gotten a careful read, it would be a clearer indication that my manuscript really was not publishable after all. It was not about "Not right for us." It was that the manuscript was really and truly bad and no publisher in North America would ever publish it, as the prophet of the famous New York agency had foretold.

On a random Tuesday afternoon in early September, I got home from school. I was going to stay only a little while, get something to eat, and head off to the university for the first meeting of my first class. I checked the mail. Nothing. No letter from M. Evans. There might have been other exciting stuff like personal letters, postcards from friends, a check for summer work, but I was singularly focused. Then I checked the one phone message: "This is Ferris Mack at M. Evans, your publisher. Give me a call."

I felt like my heart had stopped. I dialed the phone number for M. Evans and asked for Ferris Mack, who said, "we want to do your book."

I said, "I'm ready to make revisions that I'm sure you'll want."

He waited. Then he said, "Oh, we all read it around the office, and we think it's fine. Well, we want you to add a paragraph at the end because, as it is, it just sort of trails off."

I smiled and told him I could add a paragraph.

UNMAPPED TERRITORY

There is satisfaction to be had in mowing a lawn, in seeing how the untidy sweeps of grass come to clean attention with each pass, and how each pass advances the feeling of order overall. There is therapy, as well, that comes from the uncomplicated, visible, and immediate gain for time invested. Work for one hour and there is a result. Work for two hours and there are results times two.

Re-siding a house with cedar shingles is both satisfying and therapeutic in much the same ways. Such tasks can provide a counterpoint to teaching to last a lifetime. It could be enough to teach well from year to year and balance teaching's elusive rewards with the immediate, sensorial rewards of home projects. In so doing, one could happily be *just* a teacher, for a very long time.

Or one could be drawn deeper into unexplored territory that stretched in every direction from the safe and lively and warm place that is the classroom. In one direction lay the prospect of writing about the ceaselessly complicated and surprising experiences that make up the work of a teacher. In another direction lay the path of further education for a doctoral degree or administrative credential. In yet another direction lay the enticing challenge of bringing change to the moving gears of the system beyond my classroom: how to foster a deeper feeling of community, how to create an ethos where students felt connected and engaged, where teachers felt connected and engaged, where the curriculum was great ideas, and projects and big questions, especially big questions.

Nailing up a row of cedar shingles offered the distinct satisfaction of a visible result, same as mowing the back yard. Such tasks offered the pleasure of physical exertion and a rhythm of work that was meditative. But these other tasks, that lay just beyond the classroom, offered uncertainty. There were odds *against* success. I knew I could mow a lawn and re-side a house. I wanted to do something I didn't know I could do, maybe even something that other people would say couldn't be done.

I was riding my bike to school one morning, my rear wheels bumping across the many divots in the sidewalk, and as I got closer, I could see into several classroom windows. Mary was removing her coat by her desk where she had just dropped her bag. Ray was pulling up the blinds. Classrooms would shortly be full of students and teachers starting their day in each other's company. There was enough familiarity and regularity in these scenes, these routines, to compensate for what adventures I might imagine, should they go awry. I reasoned that I could most likely retreat to the territory that is known if, in venturing into unmapped land, I should lose my way or my nerve.

CHAPTER 6: REFLECTION QUESTIONS

1. In what ways is teaching fundamentally mysterious?
2. Where in teaching can you expect results? What aspects of learning can be measured? What aspects can't be measured?

3. What is the link between teaching and writing? Why do some teachers aspire also to be writers?
4. In this chapter the various ways that Jim Nehring chose to supplement his teaching carried implications. In what ways does the choice of supplemental work or hobbies or creative pursuits influence your career path? How have these choices played out in your life?

SUGGESTED READING

Teachers who write about their teaching constitute a genre of many good titles. Seminal works include Bel Kaufman's, *Up the Down Staircase*, James Herndon's *The Way It's Spozed to Be* and Jonathan Kozol's *Death at an Early Age*. More recent additions include James Nehring's *Why Do We Gotta Do this Stuff, Mr. Nehring? Notes from a Teacher's Day in School* (already mentioned) and, of course, Frank McCourt's hugely successful *Teacher Man*. For teachers, or anyone, who wishes to explore writing for publication, helpful books and magazines abound. Consider *Writer's Market*, available as a hardbound book and an online subscription. Helpful magazines include *Poets and Writers*, *Writer's Digest*, and *The Writer*.

III

Resist

SEVEN

UPPITY TEACHER

For many years, Al Shanker, president of the American Federation of Teachers, wrote a weekly column for the *New York Times*. It appeared as a paid advertisement, something I'd typically skip, but Shanker was special. A brilliant labor leader, he was also a visionary, and he was unafraid to have an idea that might shatter an orthodoxy, labor or otherwise.

One column in the spring of 1988 was about a visit to a school in Germany where a team of teachers worked together with a group of students they all shared, for several years, teaching all subjects. The students were not tracked by ability. Teachers organized the day and the curriculum to suit the needs of the students and were responsible for the total education of each child. Teachers were empowered to create ways of working with their students, without an intervening bureaucracy, and they were accountable for the outcome because they could not blame a teacher who had the student the year before.

This was, to my way of thinking, a utopian ideal, and it was being done. The column appeared, as it always did, on Sunday. Monday morning, I mentioned it in the faculty room. Dick Hermann, guidance counselor, said, sure he'd sign on for that. Others said the same thing.

I asked for a meeting with the newly hired superintendent of schools, Paul Branson, who had struck me as a teacher first and organizational leader second. He liked the idea, and being an organizational leader, pointed out that if such a thing were to become a reality, there would need to be widespread support. He asked who else was interested. I thought for a moment. Dick Hermann, I offered. Branson raised an eyebrow.

But Paul wanted to shake things up, and he saw me as a useful agitator in the teaching ranks. Also, he believed in ideas, questions, and the power of dialogue. We spoke more. He suggested a book study group. It could meet during the summer. Any interested teachers could join.

There had been a litter of books about high school reform published during the last five years by well informed, and readable scholars: Theodore Sizer, Jon Goodlad, Mortimer Adler. There were also several recent education reports: "A Nation at Risk" from a panel appointed by Ronald Reagan, as well as a visionary "blueprint" document created by the state teachers union. Shortly, a call went out to the professional staff of the district to join the summer reading group. Paul offered to pay participants for their time on site—five mornings. The group would deliberate and produce a report of their conclusions.

Come June, there were a dozen reasonably enthused enrollees, including teachers, principals, and guidance counselors. One union stalwart had joined, then dropped out before we began when he learned that pay would cover meeting time only, not time spent reading—further evidence of the deceptive tendencies of the new superintendent, who, according to the old guard teachers, was "a snake."

That summer, we took turns leading the discussion. We stayed close to the texts, mining the wisdom they offered and always returning to the question, how does this text speak to our work as educators in our schools and our district? At the end of the five mornings, which had been spread across two weeks to allow ample time for reflection between sessions, we had a stack of notes on school governance, curriculum and instruction, mission and vision, and so on.

Members were tasked with composing a section each, and I would serve as editor. Our report would be a think piece for the professional staff across the district, which, we hoped, would lead to change. The report got written, produced in an attractive format, distributed to the entire staff, and discussed with varying levels of enthusiasm.

At about this time, my book was published. It got lots of reviews, all positive. I was invited to do an interview on National Public Radio. Then CNN called, and I appeared on a talk show. The book went into a second printing, and a paperback edition was set to appear the following year. All of a sudden, I was a little famous.

One day, I was visiting the town library. I was chatting with Marvin, the librarian, and all of a sudden, like he just remembered something important, he said, "Hey, I saw your name on the banned books list."

"What?" I said, looking up from the zipper on my jacket I was fiddling with.

"I meant to tell you as soon as I saw you."

"What did you say?" I asked blinking and holding the zipper idly.

"So, every year the American Library Association publishes a list of all the books that have been banned or challenged somewhere in the United States, you know, by school districts or civic groups."

"Really?"

"Yes, and your book was listed because they didn't want it in the library in Pocatello, Idaho."

"Really. Pocatello, Idaho?"

"Yes, I think the reason was vulgar language. Wait a minute. I'll get the list."

Apparently, I was also a little infamous.

Meanwhile, other issues were competing for the attention of teachers and school principals. At the high school, the main discussion was whether to combine the two faculty rooms at opposite ends of the building into a single, centralized faculty suite. The school was a sprawl of wings and gymnasiums hooked around parking lots and vacant "courtyards." It took ten minutes to walk from one end to the other. Interestingly, this was never an issue when students complained that they couldn't go to the bathroom or get to class on time. But in the matter of combining faculty rooms, it was a major consideration. Agnes Beacham argued, "Half of my one prep period each day would be consumed by walking all the way across the building and back." She said this in a huff, the way she said most things.

One morning, I walk into the south faculty room at my end of the building. The regular crowd is engaged in the usual stuff. Five teachers, the old timers, are seated at a table leaning over their coffee, catching a few minutes of peace before pushing their kayaks into the white water that is a day of school. Larry is cursing the ditto machine. It is an era when the ditto machine is still on active duty in faculty rooms across America. There is a copy machine, too. But force of habit and memos from above saying how teachers should not abuse their copy machine privileges helps keep the ditto machine in business.

Larry has purple ink on his fingers, and there's a wrinkled, torn ditto master stuck to the drum. Loose papers, smeared with what was supposed to be the worksheet that would anchor his day, lay all about him on the counter and the floor. Martha, the home economics teacher, sits alone at a little table next to the wall. Back straight, she primps her hair, tears open a sugar substitute packet and pours it into her coffee, then stares straight ahead briefly, as if offering a silent prayer, and lifts her coffee. Mary and Lucy are absent from their sometimes table, which is where I go any morning I have a few minutes. Today, I have a few minutes.

The choices are sitting with Martha, the old timers, or by myself. I choose by myself, but near enough to the old timers to overhear the morning scuttlebut. I sit and they stop talking. I act natural, unfold the newspaper I carried into the room, spread it out on the table and look over the front pages. Talk resumes, Bill is going to the Superbowl. The talk is too eager, there's a little too much joviality. With the summer study group, the report that came out of it, and publication of my book, I am viewed in some quarters as an "uppity teacher." I am not quietly assuming my role in the classroom, I am not showing sufficient deference to the teachers who have taught more years than I in the system, and, worst of all, I am not minding my own business.

People who study the culture of schools say that, for teachers, the fundamental principles are seniority, egalitarianism, and autonomy: 1) If you've got more years in the system, your opinion counts for more; 2) no one is better than anybody else; 3) nobody tells you what to do.

PHOTO SHOOT AND PHONE JACK

Alan Shaw, a writer at *Albany* magazine, said they wanted to do an article about me. With my book just out, I was, apparently, newsworthy. I gave Alan directions to my classroom. Sure enough, he found his way to the second floor, back of the building. He poked his head into the room. "Are you Jim?"

"That's me," I said cheerily from the far side of the room where I was organizing student handouts on the counter. Alan stepped into the room, but it wasn't just Alan. With him came an entourage, a virtual to-go portrait studio; what appeared to be a photographer, because she was giving directions to the others, and two minions bearing black luggage-like boxes.

"You always travel so light?" I sassed.

They dropped their boxes on several student desks at one end of the room and began to open them and pull out a mass of black wires, shiny metal light shades with clamps, and more than one camera nestled in soft gray foam. They even brought a stool, which the photographer, Kate, sat me in, arranging my shoulders, knees, and chin into various unnatural angles that, apparently, were the only way to make the picture appear natural.

Then came the action shots: me at the board with chalk, me seated at my desk looking up at the camera, me opening the top drawer of the file cabinet. To complete the movie-set effect, the two assistants hovered continuously at Kate's side holding superwatt light bulbs aimed at my face and folding panels with shiny surfaces that amplified the already blinding light. The photo crew finished, packed up, and left while Alan and I sat at two desks facing each other and did the interview.

The October sun was descending on the other side of the building and, through my bank of windows, I could see the tree line across the field lit up while the green-brown playing field lay in the shadow of the school. Alan asked easy questions: Why did I go into teaching? What do I love about teaching? What is hard about teaching? Why did I write the book? What has changed in my life because of the book? What do my students think about the book?

But here's what I remember about that experience: just as Kate was taking a shot with me on her stool, facing the doorway into the hall, with her camera on auto-fire going *chika-chika-chika,* and the two assistants holding up a theater worth of stage lighting in their outstretched arms, Ray Vogel walked by in the hallway. He looked into my room as he passed and our eyes met. There I was, the center of a swirl of attention, in the middle of my big, bright, fashion shoot, in deep violation of rule one of the code of teachers: remain anonymous; don't stand out. After our eyes met, Ray looked away, and maybe I imagined it, but I think he shook his head ever so slightly.

Around the same time that October, I became curious about the little electrical box on the wall right next to my door. It had a phone jack in it, which I had always assumed didn't work. What if it did? One day, I brought in an old phone from home and stuck the plug into the jack. I got a dial tone. I called home, the phone rang, the answering machine picked up.

To understand my excitement at what, under normal circumstances, would be a very unsurprising discovery, you have to appreciate that no school teacher I have ever known from the pre-cell phone era had a phone in his or her classroom. In most schools, there was a one-way PA system, derisively called the squawk box because at inopportune moments it would squawk: "Will Reynold Prescott please come to the Main Office? Reynold Prescott to the Main Office immediately. Your mother dropped off your lunch. Thank you."

Say you're teaching *Of Mice and Men,* and you've just gotten to the part where Lenny gets shot by his best friend. There's an unusual kind of silence in the classroom. Students are moved, stunned, stricken even, by the weight of this poignant moment. Crackle, squawk: "There's a maroon Chevrolet Chevette in the parking lot with its lights on. License plate LZ82M. That's a maroon Chevrolet Chevette. License LZ82M. Your lights are on. Thank you." Click, squawk.

So when I plugged in my phone and got a dial tone and then called home, it was a little like the way Marconi must have felt with the first cross-Atlantic transmission. I could have a phone in my classroom. I did have a phone in my classroom. I could sit at my desk in my classroom and place a phone call. I could call the parent of a student just to say how well she was doing, or I could place a call to the parent of a student who was being inappropriate. And I could place the call at the moment of inappropriateness and invite the parent to speak with the student right then and there. I never actually did the latter, but I did get a long wire from Radioshack, which I stapled to the wall just above the baseboard and led to the back of the room and up to the top of my desk where I placed a telephone.

One day after school, I was talking on my phone from behind my desk at the back of the room. The door to the hall was open, and I could look out into the hall, which I was idly doing while talking. At that moment, Ray Vogel happened to walk by. He looked ever so briefly into my classroom to see me, chatting genially on my personal telephone. In the millisecond when he looked away before he disappeared from view, I think he shook his head.

Next morning, Trevor, the old-school English teacher next door, and a regular at the old-timers table in the faculty room with Ray, strolled over to my doorway where I was standing before first period. The hall was full of kids and noise.

Trevor said, innocent-like, "I hear you have a phone."

I said, "I do." Then, "And you can, too." This is not what Trevor was anticipating.

"How's that?" Trevor asked.

"Don't you have an electrical box at the front of your room with a phone jack in it?"

"I don't know," he said.

"Let's go look," I said and gestured for us to stroll back to his room.

This is not how Trevor imagined this conversation would go. I'm sure he imagined I would be exposed for getting special treatment from the principal for being an author or leading a summer seminar or being the superintendent's pet teacher. All of a sudden, it seemed, we were in league, searching for another cache of the buried treasure I'd found in my classroom.

We got to his door, and he gestured for me to enter the classroom first, in hopes that a mask of formality might ward off any feelings of alliance. I stepped into his room, which was a carbon copy of my own. I turned to the right and looked at the wall next to the door where there was indeed a switch plate. Trevor was now standing beside me. I looked at the switch plate, and, sure enough, right in the middle was a phone jack.

"Trevor," I said, still looking at the phone jack, "You go home, detach one of your phones from the wall, bring it in here, and plug it in." I turned my head and looked Trevor in the eye for full dramatic effect. "I'll be damned if you don't get a dial tone."

I don't usually talk like that, but I couldn't resist. Trevor's jaw was working a little, but no words came out. A few days later, I noticed there was a phone hanging on the wall right over that switch plate in Trevor's classroom. This fact dulled somewhat the incipient narrative that wanted so badly to be told in the faculty room of the uppity young teacher who was getting special privileges. It seemed that anyone who had a phone jack in their room could plug in a phone. Interestingly, I wasn't aware of anyone but Trevor and me who went and did it.

COPY ROOM ENCOUNTER

One day after school I was in the faculty work room (the new, single, unified faculty work room) making copies of a handout for my lesson on Japan's long era of isolation, which ended with American gunboats arriving in Tokyo Harbor in the 1850s. The textbook called this, "The U.S. Opens Japan" like you would open a can of tuna or a jar of peanut butter.

I was musing on this specific choice of words, counting along silently with the digital counter on the machine—37, 38, 39 . . .—when Karnie Ricardo marched into the room. Karnie brimmed with energy, like a horse in the staging pen about to be released into the rodeo arena. He was a moody guy, either smiling and roaring through a room or storming and roaring. Today, thankfully, he was smiling.

Karnie was a teacher's teacher. He had no time for administrators, education professors, state bureaucrats, and parents. He had time for students as long as they met his expectations (obedient, dutiful, uncomplaining). Karnie walked briskly into the room, stopped, and turned when he got to the far wall, like he needed the length of the room to land. He taxied over to the copy machine holding some papers, which presumably, he meant to copy. When Karnie entered a room, his energy was so palpable, everyone else in the room would begin to vibrate. The mood of the room would change, depending on Karnie's mood. I was vibrating over by the copy machine. I turned, "Hi, Karnie."

"How goes it, Dr. Nehring?"

He started calling me doctor after my book was published. For Karnie, this was not a term of endearment. In Karnie's world, being an author placed me one half-step outside the teacher clubhouse. Karnie was smiling now, an impish smile, a slightly taunting smile.

"I'm almost done. Just 30 copies to go." The counter clicked—68, 69, 70.

"You know, " Karnie started. He was standing at the end of the machine facing me. "You know the only reason you're on that board?" Karnie was referring to the fact that I had recently been invited to serve on the editorial board of the state social studies journal, a fact that had been announced at our last faculty meeting. Coming from Karnie, this was a combination question, taunt, and conversation-starter.

"Something tells me you already know the answer to that question," I said.

"Well, I know I have an opinion about it." Karnie was drawing back his full-on assault.

"Do tell," I said.

Karnie seemed knocked a little off balance by my response. He must have been expecting resistance. He turned and faced me squarely. I stayed aimed at the copy machine, trying hard to act casual.

"The only reason you have been invited to serve on that board is because you are their token teacher."

My copy job was done so I lifted the copy machine lid and scooped up my original, then looked over at Karnie. "You really think that's the whole reason?"

"Absolutely."

I waited a beat and held his gaze. "Well, then, thanks for the advice."

Karnie wasn't going to leave me alone. "Do you think there's some other reason?"

I pondered my options and said, "No. I'm sure you're right."

I picked up my copies from the output tray and said, "Machine's all yours," and walked out of the room. Was Karnie right? I wondered. Was I the token teacher chosen to make their board look like it was connected to the classroom? Or was my new status as an author an opportunity to give voice to the many voiceless teachers who work day in and day out with students? Did my presence on the board mean, in fact, that they now *were* connected to the classroom, like it or not? Maybe all of it was true, I decided. And maybe, regardless of the motives of others, I could make what I wanted of these new opportunities that were coming my way.

HALL DUTY DEBATE

Meanwhile, there was Edward Sorensen, math teacher. Tall and lean at sixty years old, he had a full head of close-cropped hair, most of which stood straight up. Like other senior teachers, Edward had his own compact analysis of what was wrong with schools. It was, to Edward, a simple and elegant theory that explained so much. And, conveniently, got him and his colleagues off the hook. Edward was happy to share his theory with anyone at any time and often did. He caught me in the hall one day as I was walking by.

"Jim!" he exclaimed from a desk positioned at the junction of two hallways where he was posted on hall duty. Edward spoke in exclamations, even when he was asking a question.

I was walking toward him and was just about to make the turn, hoping to avoid conversation. I was on my way to the library to check out a filmstrip during my prep period. Yes, filmstrip, in a spool, with a perforated edge. You feed it through a projector turning the little knob attached to a gear that catches the perforated edge. It was the 1980s.

"Edward!" I exclaimed back. I kept walking and was starting to think he'd called to me just to say hello.

"Do you have a second!" he called.

"Sure." I crossed the hall. Though perpetually exclamatory, Edward was friendly.

"Jim!" He repeated my name in the way some people will to show warmth.

"Yes, sir." I said. 'What's up' is not something you would say to Edward. He was too old-school for that, too formal.

"I've been thinking, with this committee you have for school reform, is there a way to use it to go after the number one problem with schools today?"

"Which problem is that?" I turned to face out toward the hall so I was side-by-side with Edward. We were, in effect, both on hall duty, taking watch at our post.

"Permissive parents!" exclaimed Edward, spitting the Ps. "There is a pervasive permissiveness that prevails in society today that was not prevalent in my day, and, I dare say, yours neither!"

I took my eyes off the hall and looked over at Edward, who always looked like he was standing on his heels even when he was sitting down. I pondered my options, something I found myself doing increasingly in conversation with some of the older teachers.

"So, what do you think we can do with our committee?"

"Well, you can use it to educate them! You can send home flyers that teach parents how to discipline their children, when to punish them, when to offer rewards and praise, and . . ." Edward got suddenly excited, like he'd just remembered something important. "And how to stop worrying about 'self esteem' and all that psycho-babble."

I sometimes didn't know what to say to my colleagues.

"Hmm," I said as though mulling over Edward's suggestion. "Well, I was thinking we might expand the committee to *include* parents. So, instead of sending home flyers, we could speak with them directly. We could tell them our thoughts, and they could tell us theirs. We might both learn something."

"All right then, Jim!" Edward paused, slightly unsure of himself. "I guess I need to get some work done," he offered, not in an unfriendly way. It was as though he'd just been bonked in the head and needed to recover. It was as though he had just been confronted with an argument that made sense, but he did not want it to, could not let the opinion in, because it would spread like a virus through a lifetime of carefully constructed defenses against change, leaving him unprotected. Or maybe it was that my comment revealed a gulf between our two perspectives that was far too wide to bridge, so Edward decided to give up talking about it.

"Good talking with you, Edward," I said and headed down the hall.

There was a rift opening up between me and some of the other teachers. My actions were not conforming to the easy-going, bike-riding, leather briefcase-toting mensch. A friend once told me, "If you're going to make trouble, make sure it's the right kind of trouble."

I was certain the status quo was mostly wrong. The question was, what kind of trouble was I making?

CHAPTER 7: REFLECTION QUESTIONS

1. What are the possibilities and limitations of a book-study as a strategy for change?
2. Why is there an unwritten rule that forbids teachers from doing anything that would call attention to themselves? What happens if you break this rule? What is the impact of the rule on teaching and learning?
3. How do you manage a difficult colleague like Karnie Ricardo?
4. What do you do when a friendly, senior colleague expresses a view fundamentally different from your own?

SUGGESTED READING

The mid-1980s are seen as an important moment in education when a spate of books and reports called attention to underlying issues. To get a flavor for the era read "A Nation at Risk: The Imperative for Educational Reform" from the National Commission on Excellence in Education. Essential reading also includes three books, each of which is based on a careful and broad-based examination of schools. They are *A Place Called School* by John Goodlad, *High School* by Ernest Boyer, and *Horace's Compromise: The Dilemma of the American High School*, by Theodore Sizer.

EIGHT

SCHEDULING WILL NOT BE A PROBLEM

The idea was to arrange the school's schedule so that one group of students would have English with Mary during second period and social studies with me during third period, while another group of students would have social studies with me during second period and English with Mary during third period. We also wanted to have a similar pairing of teachers and students for Jill (social studies) and Lucy (English). Arranging fifty students to have two classes back to back would be a small demand on the master schedule, but it would allow some exciting educational possibilities.

In her English class, Mary could mention history topics taught by me. In my class, I could mention books, characters, and language arts topics taught in Mary's English class. Learning in one class would be reinforced by learning in the other. That was the simplest benefit. By planning together, we could design curriculum to overlap.

Jill and I would teach about European imperialism in Africa, while Mary and Lucy would teach the novel *Things Fall Apart* by Nigerian exile Chinua Achebe about the Africans' experience of imperialism. If Jill and I needed a longer class period one day to conduct a simulation game about the stock market that took ninety minutes, students could stay with us for a double period and another day, they could spend ninety minutes with Mary and Lucy. If we wanted to invite a guest speaker to be followed by small group discussion, we could bring all 100 students to the Little Theatre to hear the presentation, then break out into four discussion groups.

The fact that we were sharing students meant we could talk with each other about them:

Me: "I noticed Henry was having trouble organizing his thoughts for the essay about the Revolutionary War."

Mary: "I've found that if I talk with Henry first about what he is thinking of writing, he's more able to put his thoughts on paper in a coherent way."

Me: "I'll try that."

We had discussed the idea with Jay, our principal, and he was on board. He assured us the scheduling would not be a problem. He gave us two days each of paid curriculum time over the summer. The course outlines would remain the same, since students were not electing the paired course sections, but the opportunity to weave courses together could be fully exploited.

On the morning of the first day of school in September, we were excited to be standing on the threshold of our great change. By the afternoon, we were still excited, but our excitement was dampened by a glitch. Several students in each class had scheduling problems. It seemed that the placement of chorus and band in the master schedule prevented them from taking a math course that was offered only during our double block. On the second day, we learned several more students had to switch out of one of the paired classes because they were unable to fit their twice-a-week science lab anywhere else in the schedule.

On the third day, there were rumblings in the faculty room:

"Did you hear about this interdisciplinary program? I didn't know anything about it."

"This didn't go to the curriculum council for approval."

"They're doing it without telling the students or their parents."

"I heard that parents had to sign up special for it. What about everyone else?"

By the end of the week, students were confused.

"How come I have to be in 3rd period English, what's wrong with 7th period?"

"Why can't they just move band?"

"So, we get to watch the whole movie?"

"We have to do double social studies?"

"I've been moved five times in four days."

Early the next week, Mary, Lucy, Jill, and I met. We agreed the new schedule was a mess, and we agreed that the prospect of getting it cleaned up anytime soon was bleak. We agreed that in the meantime, students were starting to feel confused and uncomfortable by all the schedule changes that seemed to accomplish nothing. So at the end of the day on Tuesday, we marched down to Jay's office and suggested that he give up trying to make it work.

Jay had been trying to make it work, shuttling between the guidance office and the band leader, on the phone with department heads, and talking with parents who were beginning to wonder what was going on. He was on the phone when I peeked into his office. He put a finger in the air—just a moment. The group of us waited in the hall outside his office.

A moment later he called me in. He didn't know it was the four of us. We came through his door and he looked stunned in a haggard sort of way.

I explained that we felt enough was enough. We needed to call off the new schedule for now and regroup later. I detailed all the issues that he was already quite familiar with. The solution would be to simply stop changing student schedules to force-fit the program, and we'd teach the classes just like all the rest of the faculty. There were simply no openings for the innovations we'd planned.

There followed an extended period of silence on the subject of "school reform" among those of us who sometimes talked about it. We went about our business teaching our classes, reading student papers, refilling our mugs with coffee, and generally kept our heads down.

GO BIGGER, NOT SMALLER

One October afternoon, about an hour after the school day had ended, I was sitting at a table in the faculty room by myself reading through a stack of short papers from my ninth graders on China's one child policy. All of a sudden, Lucy breezed into the room like she'd just arrived at school, ready for a day of work.

"Hi, Jim."

She swooshed past me into the adjacent copy room. Soon the copy machine was making its rhythmic *ka-chun, ka-chin, ka-floop-toop.* I concentrated on my stack of papers, trying hard to make sense of Tracy Kimball's suggestion that the United Nations set a quota each year for the number of children each country can have.

"Hi." It was Lucy again, who had left the copy machine to do its work.

"Hi. How's life?"

"You know, there's a lot that's really good that goes on inside many classrooms in our school," Lucy said.

"Uh huh," I said and held my pencil in mid-air.

"Not *every* classroom."

I didn't say anything. I was waiting for the "but" part of this comment, which seemed due right about now.

"But," Lucy paused. "It's like there's no glue that binds it all together. I mean, we have course sequences and all, but I mean, from where a student stands, how does this all come together? It doesn't. It's all just sort of random."

"Yup."

"So we tried our little experiment to make it less random, to make some kind of connection between what happens in one classroom and another, and the system chewed us up and spit us out."

"Indeed."

We both sat quietly.

"That's just what's on my mind, that's all." Lucy said and paused. "So what are you reading?"

"One child policy. Tracy Kimball says the UN should set quotas for every country, so many children per country. She writes, 'Each year, countries would be graded for how kind they've been to other countries, and they would be told how many children they can have.'"

"Go, Tracy," Lucy said.

I said, "So maybe if the system chews us up and spits us out . . . maybe we just need to break away from the system." It was a thought I'd been having recently.

"You mean go teach in a private school?"

"No. I mean if we can't do something a tiny bit innovative within the master schedule, we should go outside the master schedule. I mean that instead of just trying to do a couple courses on our own, we do all the courses on our own with a dedicated group of students. Do you remember that Al Shanker piece about the German school that was circulating about a year ago?"

"I do."

"You remember how it was a group of five teachers, and they were responsible for the whole program for about a hundred students?"

"So it would be like a middle school team?" Lucy asked.

I was reaching for something exotic, like German school reform. "Okay, like middle school. In any case, instead of getting smaller with our effort, we go bigger."

READY, SET, GO! SORT OF . . .

I asked to meet with the superintendent. I described to him the vision of a school within a school that would be programmatically separate—so as not to disrupt the master schedule—but share the real estate of the high school with other programs. Paul responded with, "Where's the support?" So I went out in search of the support.

I met with the union leaders and asked if we could survey the high school teachers to see if there was interest in exploring the idea of creating an experimental high school program. We did the survey. Not only was there interest, there were volunteers who would serve on a design team. One caveat: the teachers must vote in the majority to approve any program before it was implemented. Fair enough.

I went back to Paul, who didn't like the idea of teachers voting, but since I had brought him the expression of support he'd asked for, he couldn't very well say no. Well, he could, but he didn't. Next came funding. We needed some money, not much, but enough to pay the design team, cover their travel costs to interesting schools in the region, and buy food and supplies for meetings.

Paul suggested I meet with Mark, who was head of a well-regarded innovation center tucked in the hills outside of Albany. Mark liked the idea enough to invite me to lunch with a funder. We had lunch, and the funder said yes to a matching gift. That's when Paul and I started going door to door to key businesses in town connected with large, well-known corporations that had deep pockets. Then, at Paul's suggestion, we formed a community advisory team, which included parents, students, community representatives, and local business people.

Mark facilitated these meetings expertly. I watched and learned. Then we took all the teachers who said they were interested in joining a committee and formed three design teams. We gave them each the same specs for an innovative school-to-be, and said go forth and design something. Teams worked independently, but were encouraged to raid each other's ideas and share what they learned during visits to innovative schools in the region.

We met periodically to give each other updates. At the end, each team presented their design, and we voted. We chose one for its fundamentals, then grafted on portions of the other two that we liked. Our design was complete and we moved to the next phase, which was implementation at the high school. This meant talking about who would teach in the new program, what classrooms would be used, how we would recruit students, and how the program, though largely separate from the high school, would interface with it.

In the course of figuring out these many details, the union recommended the establishment of an "Impact Committee" to make sure it was not reducing jobs or increasing class size, etc. Then we had to have the faculty vote, which was preceded by multiple presentations and many, many informal conversations in the hallways, faculty workroom, and cafeteria. The faculty voted: three-fourths in favor and one-fourth opposed. About as good as it gets in the fractious world of high school faculty politics.

Then we began recruiting students. We needed ninety students to run the program as designed. We got fifty-four. The four teachers who'd elected to teach in the Lab School hunkered down. We were committed to seeing our new school go forward, so we figured out how we could start with just fifty-four students by having the teachers teach part time in the new program and part time in the regular high school program.

As enrollment grew over several years, we would shift to full time. Then, several union stalwarts said, *not so fast*. They said the new program was substantially different from the original program, and the faculty should once again vote.

The faculty voted again, and the result was forty-three to forty-two. We had our school by the narrowest of margins.

CHAPTER 8: REFLECTION QUESTIONS

1. Teacher reformers often complain that the school's master schedule is a huge roadblock for any innovation that extends beyond a
   single classroom. Why is it a roadblock? How do you overcome it?
2. How do the dynamics of innovation play out in this chapter? What
   similar experiences have you had with innovation? How have they
   turned out? What did you learn?

SUGGESTED READING

There are book aisles full of titles on school reform and how to change the
system. Most offer superficial strategies. Several, however, get at the
deeper issues of beliefs and attitudes, which are fundamental to change.
In particular, consider reading *The Human Side of School Change: Reform,
Resistance, and the Real-Life Problems of Innovation* by Rob Evans, *The New
Meaning of Educational Change* by Michael Fullan, and *The Predictable Failure of Educational Reform* by Seymour Sarason.

NINE

CIRCUIT TEST

Will Lab School work? That's what our pioneering students and parents wondered. Would students learn? Would there be a fixed routine? Would students move toward graduation with predictable benchmarks? Would they graduate? Would colleges accept them? Would they *succeed* in college? Would it all be different and better than school as we knew it?

The fifty-four families that signed up the very first year were collectively holding their breath and hung on every school event as a possible sign. In our second year, the first year we had seniors, college angst heightened the urgency of these questions. Then, lo and behold, a letter arrived one day in the mail for Christopher Generoso informing him that he had been accepted to Western New England College. It was as though a circuit test had just been performed, and the light bulb at the far end of the circuit lit. Lab School worked.

We started with five teachers. The school day consisted of a double period of humanities, a double period of Science, Math, and Related Technologies or S.M.A.R.T, a period of Spanish or French, then Physical Education and one elective (which was taught by teachers in the "regular" school). Every week we had a community meeting for all students and teachers, and we had a project block for the semester-long theme-based research that students carried out in small teams.

The ideas behind Lab School were everything the larger, conventional high school was not. Our courses were interdisciplinary and "real world" so students could experience learning as an inter-connected process. Work was project-based so that students could see learning as something they created, something they took control of, and something that engaged them. Assessment was based on the projects themselves, instead of tests.

We wanted our students to learn a much wider range of skills and dispositions than could be measured with multiple choice questions, short answer responses, and on-demand, generic essays. Also, students could revise their work. They could use the feedback on the first draft to make it better with the second draft. Finally, we were committed to operating as a community. We believed that when people feel a part of something, they care. And when they care, they work hard. A deliberate focus on community also fostered responsibility.

At the time, state exams, which were later to become mandatory for all students in New York, were optional. If a student wanted a "Regents" diploma, she had to take the battery of Regents exams. This was considered by many to be the gold standard. Unfortunately, it greatly constrained the educational experience, turning it into a content heavy, test prep regimen.

Alternatively, a school could offer a non-regents diploma, conferring less prestige, with a less demanding curriculum. Typically the non-regents diploma was made available to students who viewed themselves or whom the school viewed as not up to the rigor of the Regents diploma. We took the non-regents path, but for a different reason. Our gamble was to use the freedom to create an educational experience that was intellectually *more* powerful. That gamble was taken up by Harry Rosenfeld.

OUR SCARY VISITOR

He arrived just minutes before the scheduled presentations were to begin. An ancient leather briefcase hung from his left arm. He walked across the room with purpose and the measured gait of an older man. As I rose from where I was seated at the examiner's table, he looked up and met my gaze with barely a change in expression. We exchanged greetings and he quickly took his place at the table next to me.

The editor-in-chief of the Albany *Times-Union* had, contrary to prediction, accepted our invitation to serve on the board of examiners for our mid-year presentations. At mid-year and again at the end of the school year, Lab School students prepared a research project which they submitted as a paper and presented before an audience of students and family, and a panel of judges, including teachers and outside experts. Each student worked in a group of five. The group chose a theme and each member developed a project related to the theme and presented it.

Mr. Rosenfeld watched as Craig Mooney presented a research project on hemoglobin, involving some hand-drawn posters. Craig paced vigorously, like an overwrought professor, while his group-mates looked on anxiously. It would be their turn soon. A shirttail escaped Craig's belt and a thick strand of hair mostly covered his left eye. Craig explained the chemical makeup of hemoglobin, it's function as a clotting agent, it's genetic markers, and stories of intermarriage in European royal families that resulted in incidents of hemophilia.

Mr. Rosenfeld watched silently, occasionally looking down to write a note on the assessment form we'd given him. He showed no expression, at least not when I stole a glance to see what he was up to. Next, Amy Kolodny presented her group's theme of blood with a vampire twist. Tall and slender in a black business suit, Amy clicked ably through a series of PowerPoint slides all about vampire myths in Eastern Europe in the nineteenth century. The vampire stories had become a literary genre, she explained. Bram Stoker wrote the classis *Dracula* in 1897. Amy offered an analysis of the appeal of vampire stories: patriarchal fears in Victorian England, sublimated fear of Cold War spies, terrorist threats in the modern world.

Next, Alex Feldman shared his thoughts on insulin. An insulin-dependent diabetic, Alex tracked his blood sugar level, diet, exercise, and insulin injections over a three-week period and analyzed the results in order to make recommendations for how best to manage his disease. Alex was all about the details, with posters displaying charts and tables and graphs.

While the presentations induced anxiety, the real drama came with the examiners' questions, which could be directed to everyone in the group or a single student.

Mr. Rosenfeld began, "I'd like you to tell me one idea you had during your project that you did not read in a book." Silence at the student table. Kerry looked at Alex. Craig looked at Amy. Amy looked straight ahead at Mr. Rosenfeld and said, "I'll take that." She looked down then sat up straight. "So, as I said in my presentation, the ideas about Victorian fears and Cold War fears I read about, but the idea about fear of terrorists, I made up myself because it just makes sense. The thing that vampires have always been to a society has been like the big thing that a society is afraid of. In the Cold War it was a fear that the person next door was actually a Russian spy. Now that the Cold War is over, we have to find something else for vampires to represent. That's why I say terrorists because that's the thing that everyone is afraid of today."

"How about the rest of you?" said Mr. Rosenfeld, moving quickly on from Amy to whom he may have given a nod. He looked down and marked his paper. Amy looked at me. I smiled.

Craig said, "I'll answer that." My stomach tightened. "So, most people have heard about European kings and queens and inter-marriage and hemophilia and you can pretty much just look up the rest in an encyclopedia. But here's something I thought about. Most of the time, you want blood to clot. If you get a cut, you hope that pretty soon it's going to stop bleeding, right? But sometimes you don't want blood to clot. Like what if someone has a stroke or a heart attack, right? That's when blood gets stuck. So I wonder if we could figure out how to create temporary hemophilia in people so they don't get a stroke or they don't get a heart attack."

Kerry jumped in. "I've got something. We have all these charities, like the American Red Cross, and I read how they have to spend so much money on advertising and like half of all the money you donate goes to advertising and stuff." He looked at Mr. Rosenfeld for any small acknowledgement, but Rosenfeld remained poker faced. "So what if the Red Cross did a campaign where they said if you give us so much money by the end of the year, we will reduce our advertising by 10 percent next year and put that much more of your donations into our work?" Kerry said. "That way people would give them more money, and more money would go to good stuff instead of TV ads."

It was Alex's turn. There was no requirement that everyone on the team answer every question, but if Alex was going to say something, now was the moment. "I have an answer, too," said Alex, raising his hand nervously. "I suppose you could say my whole thing is an original idea." Alex paused and looked around. "I'm a type 1 diabetic. I have to have an original idea every day if I want to keep on living."

He turned and looked at Harry Rosenfeld. "Mr. Rosenfeld, you asked 'what's an original idea' I had during this project. Well, one original idea I had was that if I eat one slice of toast in the morning, my blood sugar is stable. If I eat two slices, it gets thrown off. That's an original idea. I did not understand that before I did this project. Here's another original idea. I found that if I eat five small meals during the day, instead of three big ones, my system responds much better. I found that I tolerate grapefruit juice much better than orange juice. I discovered that whole wheat spaghetti doesn't spike my system the way regular, white flour spaghetti does. I could go on. Like how almonds are more tolerable than peanuts, how dry roasted almonds are worse. I found that the opportunity to study my own disease systematically during this project shed a whole new light on the ways I can manage my diet and be healthy. So those are just some ideas I had."

The room was motionless. Somebody in the front row clapped and soon others joined in. Mr. Rosenfeld let a trace of a smile creep across his face. He nodded to Alex, and then he looked down and wrote more notes.

At the end of the morning, Mr. Rosenfeld thanked us and we thanked him. Then he left. It was unclear what he thought about the Lab School. We wondered if he would send a reporter to do a story, or maybe he would write something about his experience.

But we didn't have to wait long. That Sunday, an editorial appeared, praising the Lab School for its spirit of innovation and academic demand. In the editorial, Mr. Rosenfeld described his experience on the Board of Examiners and said that the school represented a promising direction for public education. He wrote:

Education is a major American frustration. Almost everywhere we look we find lower achievements by students and higher costs for taxpayers. . . . At Bethlehem Central High School, however, they've been doing something special about education for a couple of years. A four hour visit there last week to serve as an evaluator of student projects leaves a participant optimistic about possibilities . . . the self-supporting dynamics that emerge from students working shoulder to shoulder and meeting faculty on what appear to be more relaxed terms results in obvious accomplishments (Albany *Times Union,* January 29, 1995, page B5).

It was the sort of independent validation that was sorely needed as we continued to ride the waves of controversy within our own school district.

A REASON THEY CALL US LAB RATS

Everything we did was controversial because nearly everything we did was a tacit challenge to the mainstream. For example, we started each year with an overnight retreat to build community. While students in the main school were being lectured about new rules and new demands, Lab School students were completing a ropes course, taking communal meals, and forming research teams for the fall semester, all at a woodsy summer camp far from the drab concrete walls of school. Back home, this inspired jealousy, incredulity, and a not-so-secret hope that the Lab School would screw up, which we did, at Camp Mountain Laurel.

We'd received a letter and a bill for damages from Camp Mountain Laurel, the site of our beginning of the year retreat. Mr. and Mrs. DeGinet, the owners, had written to say that several of the bunkrooms had been left a mess and several items had been broken, including a chair and two lamps. They were charging us 133 dollars and asking us not to come back. The teachers decided to take the letter to community meeting, read it to the whole group, and ask the students what they think.

"I think we should go back for a day, the whole school, and do whatever work they need done just to show we're sorry and we want to make it right," said Danielle who was sitting cross-legged on the floor in the middle of the crowded room.

"But that's like punishing everyone because a few people did something bad." This was Ian, sitting on the counter under the bank of windows that ran along one wall. The room, a double classroom that was the Lab School's home, held all seventy-two students and four teachers, every Wednesday morning for community block, which meant planning, announcements, celebrations, and discussion of issues.

"I think they're exaggerating." This was Eric standing at the back of the room. Heads turned. "I think we didn't actually do the stuff they say

we did, and they just need money to fix stuff and so they're blaming us."
A wave of murmuring passed through the room.

"I don't think they're exaggerating," said Thomas, who was seated up
front. "You and I know what the boys' dorm looked like when we left."

"I broke the lamp," said Gordon all of a sudden, seated next to Danielle on the floor.

"Yeah, catching a Frisbee," Carl added from across the room and
laughed.

"But I cleaned up the glass and I put it back on the table. It still
worked. I didn't think much of it. I guess I should have said something.
I'll pay for it."

The room was quiet. Thoughtful.

Danielle spoke up again. "I'm worried about our reputation." Pause.
"I mean, we all know Lab School is under a microscope. There's a reason
they call us Lab Rats. Things get around. Pretty soon everyone will be
saying, 'all those lab school kids, what a bunch of losers. They all have a
big party and get kicked out of the summer camp they rented.'"

"I hardly think our retreat was a party." This was Ian on the counter
by the window.

Danielle: "I know it's not a party, and you know it's not a party, but
out there . . ." She gestured out the door to the hall. "Out there they don't
get it. They don't get *us*." Another pause. "Can we just go back? Could
we just take a day and say we'll do work, painting stuff or cleaning or
whatever they need?"

And we did. At the prompting of our students, we contacted Mr. and
Mrs. DeGinet, who were hesitant at first, but finally agreed. They gave us
a list of chores, and we organized teams. There was leaf-raking, bathroom
painting, stonewall rebuilding, weeding, and roadside litter pick up. We
all decided that we wanted to be organized about this and make a good
impression, so we set up the teams in advance and made sure that between the camp and what our students could bring from home, there
would be enough tools and supplies to get the work done. We ordered
up a school bus for the day, sent letters and permission slips home to
parents, and, day-of, every student was there on time for the bus up to
Camp Mountain Laurel.

BACK TO CAMP

"So, you want to find the right rock to fit in the space based on how the
other rocks are shaped," I told the group. One student, Sarah, and I each
had a rock the size of a casserole dish clutched in our hands. We stood
like two gorillas hunched over the partially built wall, each with a rock
hanging from our extended arms.

One of the items on Mr. and Mrs. DeGinet's list of repairs was to fill a breach in an existing wall. Someone had driven a backhoe through this spot years ago, which meant the wall had been disassembled, rocks thrown everywhere, and it was never rebuilt, until today.

I heard laughter from the cement shower house down the dirt road where a crew of five or six painted the walls with rollers and big brushes. I looked up the road the other way, and I saw Dennis, a senior, bossing around his team of sophomore and freshman boys who were raking out and weeding a big patio that had been ignored for the past several seasons. Meanwhile, Sarah had chosen a stone and was hunch-walking it over to an empty spot in the wall.

"You okay if I step away for a bit?" I asked just as Sarah stepped over the wall toward another rock.

"Fine," she said without looking up.

I stepped off down the dirt road, wondering what I would see when I entered the domain of the painting project. They were singing. "The ants go marching twelve by twelve. Hurrah! Hurrah!" I stepped around a corner of the building and came to the entrance, where I stood, unnoticed, and took in the scene. Four boys were moving as a line across the room, rolling paint across the ceiling and two boys were working each wall with wide brushes. And they were all singing. Brian saw me and called out, "Hey, Mr. Nehring." Everybody looked. The singing sputtered out.

"You guys are doing a great job. I'm trying to think what rhymes with thirteen."

"Don't worry. We'll think of something," said Michael.

LEARNING "A LESSON"

Even before we left for our return trip to Camp Mountain Laurel, the buzz around school was that in teaching our students "a lesson," we were wasting valuable learning time. This struck me as ironic. I thought that school was for lessons, that teaching responsibility was valuable learning, and that there was more to this trip than raking leaves. I decided to take up the issue in class shortly after we returned to school.

"So, what did you learn?" is the question with which I started my humanities class the following Monday afternoon. The students looked back at me from their tables, puzzled. "What did you learn from your day at Camp Mountain Laurel?"

There was a short silence and then Ian replied. "We learned that we should be respectful of other peoples' property." This was delivered in a sing-songy voice that mocked the question.

"That's not what I mean," I replied.

"So, what do you mean?"

"Earlier today, I heard some of you complaining that some of the students and some of the teachers outside of Lab School were criticizing our trip, saying it wasn't a day of learning, it was just a community service day, and fun-and-games, and it should have been done on a Saturday, right? Wasn't that the buzz going around this morning?"

"Oh yeah. Mr. Olson, he stopped me in the hall . . ." Kevin said.

"No." I said firmly to Kevin. "Stop right there. We are not talking about individuals. We're talking about an issue."

I began again. "We're going to make a list on the board of the things you did. Okay? Anyone, please just call out something that you did on Friday at Camp Mountain Laurel."

"I raked out an old patio."

"Okay," I replied and wrote on the board. "What else?"

"I painted a ceiling."

I wrote and continued, "What else?"

"I weeded for four freakin' hours," a student chimed in. I wrote and smiled sympathetically.

"I dug post holes. Fifteen post holes all in a row," said Joseph. "And they were perfect, I'll have you know. Exactly 22 inches, and. . . ."

"Got it, Joseph," I interrupted. "Thank you."

Joseph in stage whisper to the class, "I measured each one. Perfect. Twenty-two inches exactly."

"I built a stone wall," Sarah stated proudly.

We added more to the list. Then I stepped back from the white board, looked at the class, and then looked at the board. "Good list," I said. "Now I have a question for you." I looked at my class of twenty-three students. They did not look orderly. The six tables at which the students sat were not laid out in any discernible arrangement, just plunked down around the room. Some students were hunched forward on their elbows. Several, in chairs not really associated with any table, leaned back with their big adolescent legs sprawled in front. Ian and Jeremy were sitting on the counter top by the window. But they were all looking at me. And their eyes said *I'm ready, and I'm thinking. What's next?*

I began, "What's a skill you had to use on Friday?"

"So I had to paint one of the walls in the shower house," Jeremy said. "I figured I needed some kind of a system because it's this enormous wall that just goes on for like a hundred feet, but here's the thing, it's made up of all these cement blocks, so it's like a grid, like a giant piece of graph paper, you know what I mean? So I started painting in one corner and pretty quick I realize it takes me about 45 seconds to paint one block. So I count the blocks, you know height times length. So it's 15 high by 30 long. That's 450 freakin' blocks! At 45 seconds per, that came out to like five and a half hours of painting. And I was *not* going to paint for five and a half hours."

"So I figure, okay, I'm just going to keep painting and see what I can do to get the 45 seconds per down to maybe something like 15 seconds, because I figure if I can do that, then I'm talking like maybe a two hour job." Jeremy scanned the audience again. Heads nodded. "And I can do a two hour job. Pretty soon, I'm coming up with little improvements. Like I move the paint can right under where I'm painting so I don't have to move the brush as far. Then I try smooshing the brush against the wall to fill all the little cracks faster instead of just like brushing back and forth. And so I time myself for every like ten bricks, and I'm down to thirty seconds. Then I'm down to fifteen seconds."

"So how long did it take you?" asked Danielle from the front of the room.

"Took me three hours. World's most boring job." Everyone laughed.

Jana called out loudly from her table on the other side of the room, "Yeah except for pulling weeds." Heads swiveled. "I lasted an hour and then I had to quit."

Danielle, unofficial spokesperson for the group: "So you just walked away?"

"She made a deal," called Sarah from the other side of the room. Heads swiveled again.

"I'm intrigued," I said from the front of the room where I was still standing by the whiteboard holding a marker. "So you girls worked something out on your own? Sounds like you worked out some kind of creative solution. Tell us about it."

"It was me and Gina, too," added Jill.

"So it was four of you, Jana, Sarah, Jill, and Gina," I eyed each girl as I said her name. Again, I wanted them to tell their story, so I said, "What did you girls figure out?"

Emboldened, Jill began, "We were all assigned to the world's most boring jobs. Me and Gina, we had to pick up litter along that access road or whatever. It was like two miles long. We each had a bag, and we each took a side of the road, and there was a ton of garbage all over the place, under bushes, behind trees, stuck inside bushes, plastic bags like in the branches. And it was an all day job just walking along getting all the trash."

"Right, so you remember the meeting we had?" This was Jana, eager to get back into the conversation she'd started now that everyone, including the teacher, was interested. "Remember how you guys," she said, gesturing to me as the representative teacher, "had everyone all come back for like a big huddle after the first hour just to check in and make sure everything was going smoothly?"

"I do remember," I said.

"So at that little meeting, me and these guys, we're all like 'I've got the most boring job in the world' and 'no you don't, mine is worse.' So Jill over there says, look, what if we swap off, like every hour on the hour, we just rotate so we can see who's really got the worst job and so we don't all go crazy just doing the same thing all day? At first, we're kinda like 'I don't want to do your job,' but then we thought it's not such a bad idea. And then it was like a competition to see who can get the most done on each job. Then it became interesting."

"Yeah, I won," said Jill all of a sudden. "Hands down. Pulled more weeds, picked up more trash."

"No way," came the chorus back from Sarah, Jana, and Gina.

Who knew painting and weeding could spawn so much creative thinking? Such learning is hard to measure, but it's worth teaching. The education world had become so test-driven that anything untestable was getting crowded out. The Lab School was taking a stand, and in a small way, we were winning.

A RAINBOW APPEARS

By its third year, so many things the Lab School had invented on the spot in the first year had become routine. Every January and June students knew they needed to have a research project ready to present to an audience, including a panel of several peers, teachers, and at least one adult from the outside world. Every week, the whole school met for a community meeting, which was part announcements, part celebration, part forum for discussion, and part legislative body. We had classes with clear expectations and a demanding, project-based curriculum. Students regularly revised work and told us they were working harder than they'd ever worked in the traditional school, but that they loved what they were doing.

Meanwhile, a charter school movement was popping up around the country, not so much in New York State, but quite vigorously just over the border in Massachusetts. Charter schools were a new idea: autonomous public schools that answered not to a local school district, but directly to the state. And they were funded by the state on a per-pupil basis.

This seemed the purest expression of what the Lab School had aspired to carve out for itself in one small corner of a conventional high school in a conventional school district, which is why it was interesting to receive a letter from Theodore Sizer, the famous school reform leader, saying that he and his wife were involved in a brand new charter school in central Massachusetts and that I'd be welcome to visit. At the time this letter arrived, April vacation was just around the bend. Maybe the Nehring family could go on a little road trip, say, to Boston, look at the fish at the New England Aquarium, and, along the way, make a short visit. And so we did.

We spent two days in Boston viewing exotic fish with big teeth, weird antennae, and transparent skin, and one day in central Massachusetts where I visited this mysterious charter school while Laurie and the girls explored nearby Concord and Thoreau's Walden Pond.

Fast forward to the ride home on the Massachusetts turnpike, west of Worcester, pointing toward Albany and home.

Laurie: "You realize you've been talking non-stop about this charter school since you got in the car, right?"

Me: "Hmm."

Laurie: "No, I really. (Looking at watch). We've been driving for 55 minutes, and you've been gushing about this place."

Me: "I guess I have. (Pause.) There's something else."

Laurie: "Uh oh."

Me: "They're looking for a lead teacher, principal-type person. They're looking to hire someone for next year."

Laurie: "So you want to pack up and move to Massachusetts?"

Me: "They asked me if I'm interested."

Laurie: "Really?"

Me: "Really. (Pause.) But you're right. Why would we ever want to move? It's just so . . . crazy."

Laurie: "You're right."

Laurie and me: (Silence.)

Laurie: "On the other hand . . ."

We began to talk about how maybe, just maybe, moving to Massachusetts wouldn't be a *completely* crazy idea. The Lab School was almost on its feet, coming to the close of its third year in operation. Our daughters were only just starting school. If we were going to make a big move, now would be a good time.

On the other hand, Laurie would leave behind her entire professional network, which was key to the at-home business she had recently launched. We talked through the Berkshires, and as the highway descended on the far side, down into New York State, *why?* morphed into *why not?* At this point a rainbow appeared. Truly. In the sky ahead of us, on display for all to see, a real Technicolor rainbow appeared in our path.

CHAPTER 9: REFLECTION QUESTIONS

1. For Lab School, college acceptance for our seniors was a crucial benchmark of success. What are appropriate markers of success in education reform?
2. Why are pencil and paper tests the dominant mode of student assessment? What are their strengths and limitations?

3. What are the merits of a project-based curriculum? What are the merits of a juried assessment such as is featured in this chapter? What are the pitfalls?
4. How do you teach responsibility and character? Should school devote time to them?

SUGGESTED READING

In recent decades, a movement has coalesced around assessment that gets beyond pencil and paper tests in order to more deeply engage students and assess complex skills. For an introduction to performance assessment, read *Beyond the Bubble Test: How Performance Assessment Supports 21st Century Learning* by Linda Darling-Hammond. For a practical guide, see *Assessing 21st Century Skills: A Guide to Evaluating Mastery and Authentic Learning* by Laura M. Greenstein.

On the subject of character education and moral reasoning as a school priority, consider *The Students Are Watching*, by Theodore and Nancy Sizer; also, *The Moral Life of Children* by Robert Coles. Both books make a compelling case that whether schools choose to teach it, character and morality are central to the thoughts and emotional development of children. Better for schools to be deliberate in their attention to these crucial aspects of education.

IV

Deeper Learning

TEN

BORN FOR THIS JOB

They say that among life's biggest stressors are starting a new job, moving, building a new house, and bringing a child into the world. So it was that I applied for the job at a charter school, interviewed two weeks later, and landed the position. We sold our house, and I reported to work July 1. Laurie and the girls joined me in August, and soon enough we moved into our newly constructed house. In March, our third daughter, Anna, was born.

"If we have a successful four weeks of summer planning, what will we have at the end of it that we don't have right now?" This was my question to the faculty on my first day at the new charter school. Unlike most schools, the teaching staff worked for a month during the summer to plan the school year. It was the 8th of July and we would be together into the first few days of August.

"We'll have a master schedule that actually works!" Ron called out. I wrote it on the white board.

"We'll have a curriculum outline for arts and humanities for the year and a detailed plan for the first major unit," Ianna said. I wrote it on the white board.

"Ditto for MST," called Lisa. MST stood for Math, Science, and Technology.

"Lo mismo para el Español," said Rob, the lone Spanish teacher.

"We'll have some kind of a program for physical activity," said Chris.

"And we'll hire a teacher to design and lead it," added Donna.

The list went on, and I wrote and wrote. The exercise was cathartic. For a year, this stalwart group of teachers had been making up just about everything from one day to the next: a new schedule every week; experiments with curriculum, instruction, and student groupings. They longed for a chance to plan something that would last more than five days. They longed for stability, just maybe a little routine. Now, suddenly, at the far end of an exhausting year laying track inches ahead of the train, they had four weeks *sans* students to think big.

By Wednesday of our first week the tension produced from a year of deep uncertainty, combined with the necessity of being with students every day fostering something like a coherent experience, began to lift. The days rolled by and we produced unit plans and assessment rubrics, solved scheduling problems, sorted out student groupings, re-designed our use of classroom space, bought filing cabinets, organized material, and discussed individual students. We were laying track.

On Friday afternoon at the end of our second week, I was sitting in my cubicle in the Main Office.

"Jim," Rick said, leaning around the partial wall. "Got a minute?"

"Of course." I swiveled around in my chair to face Rick. "Come on in. Have a seat."

"Oh, no, that's okay. I just . . . I just wanted to say thank you."

"Well, that's nice. For what?"

"For just doing everything you've done in the past two weeks."

"I haven't done that much really, but you're welcome."

"No, you have done that much. I mean, you've really helped us pull ourselves together. You are a masterful planner and organizer of people."

"Well, I've got great people to work with."

"So, I just wanted to say thanks."

Rick left, and I turned back to my laptop. A minute later, Joseph, one of our MST teachers, appeared and professed the same message. In the course of that late Friday afternoon, six teachers stopped by to say thank you. That night, I went home and I said to Laurie, "I think I was born for this job."

FIRST DAY

Our first day of school—with students—was blessed by a clear blue sky and dry air that presaged autumn while holding the heat of summer. We gathered on the lawn in front of our school, a massive brick edifice, four stories big and as wide as a city block. A former Special Operations training center, the building was a centerpiece of the de-commissioned army base where our school community had found a home the year before. Flanking the main entrance were four large windows. Other than that, no windows. Not one, just unrelenting brick and mortar with copper mesh buried in the walls to keep out radio signals. A bulletproof guardhouse stood sentry out front.

The front lawn was filling now with a crowd of expectant parents who would linger for about half an hour for an opening ceremony before continuing on with their day. Their children, our students, stood clotted in circles of fevered conversation or darted around the front yard, fueled by first-day-of-school energy and anxiety. At the appointed hour, I gave a speech and the crowd briefly settled down. Afterwards, parents, teachers, and even some students said things to me like, "Great speech, Jim!" Our students called us by our first names.

Shortly, the parents were gone and our students were organized into small groups for a team-building experience. We had two full days of "retreat," planned in the calm of July. Once we were satisfied that students were sufficiently bonded with each other, and their new younger classmates, and their new teachers hired over the summer, and the very idea of school after two months of freedom, then, only then, would classes begin.

During the retreat, I got to play, too. This principal would be different from most. I would also teach. My title was, after all, principal teacher. For the retreat, students rotated, in small groups, through a series of activities led by individual teachers. The whole school was scattered around the lawn surrounding our massive, fortress-like building.

My assigned activity was Hot Lava. I told my group that a forty foot by forty foot square, marked off on the grass with a rope perimeter represented a pool of fiery lava. The challenge was to safely transport all members of the group across the lava. To assist in this challenge the group was given four paper plates and told that each plate represented a portable safe zone. A person would be shielded from the lava as long as he or she was standing on the plate. A plate could be positioned anywhere in the field of lava, but each person had to move through the middle of the lava pit from one end to the other without stepping off to the side.

Rory, Connor, Sarah, Malcolm, and Lisa pondered their challenge. Malcolm and Lisa were returning students. Rory, Connor, and Sarah were new to the school.

Malcolm said, "Okay, so one way would be to toss the first plate out, step on it, then throw the next plate out farther and step on it and keep going until you're across."

"Except that you'll run out . . .," said Lisa.

"Right," Malcolm said. "If it was twenty feet, we could do it."

The group was silent.

Malcolm spoke again. "What if we do angles?" His teammates looked at him curiously. "So we drop the plates part way across sort of angling over to the side. Then everyone steps off, we pick up the plates, and then we do the same thing for the second half."

Rory, a small and wiry seventh grader spoke up. "Jim said we can't step on the side."

Malcolm looked over at me. I had my sunglasses on, sitting cross-legged on the sideline to the right of the lava pit.

I nodded. Rory looked proud at being right.

After ten minutes of talking and experimenting, they figured out a system of moving plates and people that would inch them across the hot lava. The activity could have ended there and it would have been enough to build team spirit, but we, as a school, were interested in deeper learning. John Dewey said that learning does not come from experience. It comes from reflection on experience. We circled up on the lawn near our lava pit.

"So, early in the process, what was a moment that felt like a turning point to you? What was a moment that felt like something clicked?" I asked.

Malcolm spoke first. "I think the turning point was when Lisa had the idea to get us all onto the plates at once."

Lisa said, "Right, but I got that idea only because Rory started just putting us on the plates."

Rory spoke. "Yeah but then after you and me got people on the plates, Malcolm came along and figured out how we needed to stand so that we could have everybody on the plates and still have one plate left over."

"Uh huh," I said. I looked over at Conor and Sarah. "So, Sarah and Conor, you guys were a little on the quiet side, but you were still very actively involved in the work. Can you talk a little about what you were thinking during the activity?"

"Well, I didn't say anything," Conor began. "I mean I didn't say *nuthin'*!"

"Okay," I said, "So that sounds like maybe a choice on your part. Can you talk more about that?"

"Well, if everybody is leading, then there's no one to follow."

I said, "So you were deliberately letting others lead."

"Sort of."

"Okay." I added. "Interesting. And Sarah." I turned to look at Sarah, who was sitting on the other side of the circle.

"I spoke up." She said, just a bit defensively.

"You sure did," I said. "And you asked a crucial question. Who remembers the really important question that Sarah asked?" I turned to the whole group.

"I remember," said Rory. "Sarah asked what would happen if we fell off."

"Right." I confirmed. "Always a good idea to know the rules when you're walking across lava." I smiled at Sarah, who smiled back.

In that moment, I thought about everything I love about teaching.

ONE TUMBLEWEED

Our two day retreat accomplished everything we hoped. Our students were ready to engage with each other, with their teachers, and with real questions. On day three, we started school, meaning everyone moved back indoors and into classrooms following our new master schedule.

At 8:15, there was a tidal wave of students that moved through the building and then, suddenly, the hallway was quiet, almost as though the school day had just ended and not just begun. There was silence. Two girls stepped from the bathroom at mid-hall, talking energetically. Spooked by the empty hall, they realized they were late for class. They ran with small, quick steps toward their classroom. Soon I was standing in the hallway alone.

It felt like I'd arrived at the party just as it ended. I felt superfluous, with everyone but me having a place to go and a purpose to serve. I looked sideways as I crossed the first classroom and caught a glimpse, through the narrow window in the door, of three students standing in a line at the whiteboard. They were smiling. Something interesting was afoot in that classroom. I kept walking and looked into another room. This time, a teacher, Eddie, stood at the front of the room, silent and listening. Another room showed everyone seated in a circle at desks, each with the same book. Faces looked thoughtful.

I kept walking, but I stopped peering into rooms. It felt voyeuristic. In a couple of the classrooms into which I peered, people peered back. Our eye contact was so brief that no expression had time to surface and register. They were blank looks. Maybe there was a hint of surprise. I didn't want to get a reputation for staring into classrooms.

As I circled back to my office, it occurred to me that the party was not over. Rather the party was very much under way. It's just that I was not invited.

A DAY IN THE LIFE

I became a principal not because I wanted to be a principal, but because I wanted to open a space for the kind of school I desperately wanted to be part of, the kind of school I wanted as many families as possible to have access to. Leadership is the role that was placed in front of me as the means to accomplish this goal. So I stepped into it, repeatedly, as it was turning out, and I accepted the combination of adrenaline rush, disturbed sleep, and continuously gnawing worry that went with it.

But I dislike managing people. I'd rather they manage themselves. And I don't want to be responsible for their problems. And I don't like devoting huge amounts of my work time complying with directives from above and beyond. But I did the work as best I could and took from it what joy I could. I kept a diary for part of that time and my entries reflect the sheer madness of the job in the midst of our ambitious school's second year in existence.

5:00: I rise, run my two miles, get ready for school and after a stop at Dunkin Donuts—where there's already a line at 5:45, pre-dawn—I'm at Parker a little before six. I settle into my cubicle in a corner of the all-purpose Main Office/nerve center. It is, for the moment, quiet. I work first on a draft of a letter to the trustees on a proposal that the lead teachers and I have been discussing to reconfigure the lead teacher positions. Next, I work on a functional job description for myself: What does a Principal Teacher do?

7:00: I face the mountain—a one foot pile of letters, phone messages, and file folders from meetings that have accumulated on my desk over several days. My system of ensuring that things don't get forgotten is to not file them or put them on a shelf until they are done. Because I go through the pile continuously, anything that is unfinished will be excavated and either re-piled or finished. I am vaguely aware this is not a recommended managerial practice.

7:30: A man in a blazer walks into the office and introduces himself as so and so from Harvard University, here for the day. While keeping a calm exterior I mentally scramble, trying to place this visitor. He indicates that he will meet the interns (master degree candidates at Harvard who teach at Parker) when they come in (ah hah—the intern coordinator). He asks for literature on the Parker School and seems content to sit and read.

7:45: Teachers and kids start to trickle in. Roger, a student in my advisory, arrives and asks me for my keys to open up the room. I remind him that yesterday he didn't bring them back until forty-five minutes later, and I really do need to have the keys back promptly this morning. "No problem, Jim," Roger says.

Harvard is happily ensconced in standards and rubrics. Intermittently the phone rings. I generally don't pick it up before 8:00 a.m. because most calls before then are *so and so will be out with the flu today*, so I let the machine take it. Linda, our receptionist, arrives. I introduce Harvard, and Linda swings into action. Harvard number two walks in: Jennifer. Introductions. Linda says we look forward to meeting with them at ten. (Oh yes, I think. That's what Linda was talking about yesterday.) I take them on a tour of the school, and leave them with Jane, one of our Harvard intern-teachers, who asks them to sit in on advisory.

8:00: I head back to the office. The hallways are filling up. Julie, the facilitator we've hired for the upcoming trustee retreat, calls. Can we meet at 9:30 today? Yes, I say, unsure who I might have to disappoint as I reach for my calendar book. The meeting with Julie needs to be a priority.

Then I see it, the note from Seamus (Physical Activity teacher), the note from Friday that informed me that we did not have PA coverage for Monday when he would be out and that we need PA coverage again today! At the moment of this realization, Rob, one of our two Spanish teachers, appears before me. Kelly (our other Spanish teacher) will be out today, he is saying; she already called all the subs, and no one is available. We need coverage for three of her four classes.

This will be the crisis du jour. Instantly, everything on my desk moves to the back burner. I could cover PA again with some activity or other, but we'll still need Spanish coverage. What to do? I put up a note in the faculty room: "Creative Problem Solving time." I describe the situation and ask for any ideas ASAP. I run into John, a teacher, and we formulate a solution.

The Math, Science, and Technology (MST) teachers will cover PA by running their weekly staff meeting in the gym. I will teach Spanish at the end of the day. That leaves one uncovered Spanish class. Lily, our librarian, volunteers. Problem solved. I plaster a note over my earlier faculty room notice: "Problem Solved! You guys are terrific!" And I quietly regret the anxiety that this institutional dysfunction has created today, again.

8:30: Morning advisory, our daily fifteen-minute check-in. Each teacher, including me, supervises an advisory of about twelve students. I take attendance. Ian, recently back from suspension, is here today. It is odd to serve as advisor to a student that as principal teacher I have recently also thrown out of school.

We "connect," a daily ritual of personal sharing. Nice atmosphere. The kids are open, in a friendly mood this morning. I ask Ian to stay after advisory because I've been wanting to commend him for several good reports from his teachers. We talk. It lifts us both up.

8:45: Back to the office. Linda has been making phone calls to new additions to the sub list to see if anyone can take the PA classes. Dom is available. Great. MST is off the hook. They can hold their meeting undistracted.

Next in the door is our Boston College visitor, a graduate student who is part of a team studying charter schools. I briefly show her around, hoping all the while that the students will have their welcoming committee organized soon. She goes off visiting classes. Julie, the consultant, arrives. We meet and talk about the upcoming trustees retreat.

10:05: Maureen, our director of student services and liaison to the intern program, pokes her head in. Jennifer and Roy from Harvard are waiting to begin our meeting. I swing out of the conference room where Julie and I have been planning the retreat and into Maureen's office where all are assembled. We spend an hour working through issues. We agree that breaking new ground is never easy, and indeed, we are breaking new ground, exciting for both Parker and Harvard. We are making a difference together.

11:00: Time for my weekly session with Donna and Roger, lead teachers for Arts and Humanities (AH) and Math, Science, and Technology (MST), respectively. We spend an hour talking about changes to the lead teacher positions and agree to move forward. Next, I offer a recently spawned thought that all students should attend the upcoming gateways next week. The gateway is our school's student exhibition of readiness for promotion to the next division. This is a bit of a bombshell because it means yet another institution-wide disruption, but Roger and Donna nod: Yes, all students should attend the gateways, especially the new students, to acclimate them to Parker-style assessment. We work out a system to organize it.

Fifteen minutes to "Fun Lunch," and I depart the Donna and Roger meeting to write a memo to the faculty announcing that Gateways will be attended by all students and explaining how it will work and admit that it is last minute, but *carpe diem.* I distribute the memo and race to advisory Fun Lunch, which was organized yesterday, a party to which each student has brought some contribution of food or music.

12:45: (Fun Lunch) Five kids have CDs. To avoid fighting, we agree each will get five minutes of air time. This works. We eat, talk, and listen to music. Fun Lunch is a success. We clean up and before leaving I remind everyone that today is our day to clean up the lunchroom. A collective groan. We agree to do it during advisory check out.

1:15: Off to Spanish. I am covering for Kelly, doing a *Fin de Semana* skit with the level ones and then the level twos. We do our thing. The kids are impressed with the little Spanish I know. I finish the second hour elated.

3:15: Off to advisory check out. We clean the lunchroom, declare our work awesome, and the kids depart for the day.

3:30: Back to the Main Office. I am confronted with several moderate-size problems. Afternoon PA was a disaster.

4:30: The building is quiet. I'm all worn out. I have no more to give. I fumble around at my desk and throw out some papers from the mountain that are no longer relevant. I mentally sort out what I'll do from 6 to 7:30 tomorrow morning in order to be in good shape for the day. My mind is relatively clear. I can go now.

I pack up. Most others have gone. I head for the door. It's 5 p.m. College Admissions Committee meeting tonight at 7 p.m.

I spent lots of time doing things in my principal role that felt like the things a principal should do, but mostly I made it up as I went along. I had not studied to be a principal. I had no experience as a principal. I had started a small school and led it as a teacher—which is what had appealed to the people at this school about my candidacy. I would make an unconventional principal, a principal who was a teacher at heart.

And there was, despite my secret reluctance for the job (secret even to me), plenty of good principal work that got done. We came up with a master schedule that worked. This was a major accomplishment because the school had struggled to invent one that met all needs. The one we created ensured appropriate time for all classes while providing generous time in each teacher's day for meetings and individual preparation. We also took strides in developing curriculum.

By the end of our second year, we were no longer laying track just ahead of the train. We also began to solidify our Spanish program and develop "physical activity" into a wellness program with a strategic hire. The school was growing and we hired more teachers for all the domains. We were fortunate to bring aboard many fine teachers, some of whom would end up staying for years and years.

In the area of school culture we ever so slowly sorted out the norms that would govern relationships among the adults and students. We would not be a school with three-strikes-you're-out and lists of rules and tables of penalties. We would be a school with a simple expectation of respect governed by a continuous appeal to each person's dignity and moral reason. This meant lots of talk, lots of mediation, and lots of time. And, most days, we agreed, it was time and energy well spent. It was part of learning. It was part of what it is to be a school where how you treat others is part of the unwritten but not unimportant curriculum.

There was also the management side of the school: budgeting, facility, supplies, insurance, and so on. We had a very capable school manager, and we hired a very experienced financial officer. Sorting out our roles, however, was complicated. We were always stepping on each other's toes, actually, mostly me landing accidentally on other people's toes and not noticing because I was consumed with the pile on my desk and all the issues it represented, plus the teaching I tucked in on the side. What we needed was a full-time principal who truly oversaw the school, not a lead teacher who taught while attempting to direct and manage.

A ROLE MODEL, PLEASE?

If I'd had one good role model, I might have had a more hopeful and confident outlook, but recalling the principals I'd observed over the years, there wasn't much to choose from. For example, there was Michael who deflected any and all suggestions from his staff.

"Hey Michael, what if we . . ." Fill in any suggestion you care to—a new way to schedule math classes, new lunch rotation, better way to do final exams, etc. You're standing in the hallway. Michael is right next to you. You are both looking on as students change classes. Michael, a large man in his forties with a head of hair like a bristle brush, makes a quarter turn toward you. Upon barely hearing your suggestion, a bunch of words pour forth as if Michael is hastily erecting a kind of defensive wall. Then he holds up his right hand with the index finger up and pulls back the tip of it with his left hand.

"One" he says, imagine the number one with an exaggerated "O" sound. Some more words. Then he holds up the next finger and holds both back.

"Two," he says. More words. You realize he is enumerating the reasons why your idea won't work. This was Michael's standard response to a staff suggestion. It was so standard that in the faculty room, whenever anybody had an idea and talked about sharing it with Michael, someone nearby would hold up fingers, pull them back, and say, "Oone . . . Twooo."

There was also Joe, who was in his fifties, had very white teeth, and exuded the spirit of a healthy, tanned, Florida golf enthusiast. Joe came up to the principal job by way of physical education teacher, then athletic director. Though I didn't know it at the time, Joe was counting the years to retirement. He was well liked by the veteran teachers and was a good manager of budgets and schedules and a good disciplinarian in the way that many teachers want a principal to be, meaning the teacher is always right.

Joe kept the trains running on time. As far as teaching went, Joe's vision for education went as far as students paying attention, studying hard, and doing well on their tests. He conducted a formal observation of my teaching. During the de-brief he commented that I looked a little disheveled and that I might brush my hair and straighten my tie.

And there was Ron. Ron knew all the latest education talk. He had personalized stationery with his name and a motto: *a community of learners*. At the time, I didn't think much of that as a motto. Of course we're a community of learners, I reasoned, we're a school, for goodness sake. It would be like the motto of a carbonated beverage company being "soda in a bottle."

Ron did not have much fizz. When he led a faculty meeting, he addressed the assembled staff as "you-people." His commentary during faculty meetings often explored the gap between what "you-people" wanted and what "you-people" were willing to do. "You-people" want more orderly hallways, so "you-people" need to be out in the hallways monitoring them. Mary and I used to count how many times Ron said "you-people" during a faculty meeting. The record was forty-one.

And, of course, there was Vince from Middle Valley, who boot-camped kids into quivering submission with a drill sergeant vocabulary, big forearms, and bulging eyes.

Terence was an exception. He became the district supervisor of language arts after the top three candidates for the job were suddenly no longer available. Terence was all about teaching and how to foster it in the English department. He was soft-spoken and focused. Other administrators thought he would crumble, but he proved them wrong.

Terence was what the education world would later call an instructional leader because his focus was first on teaching and learning and second on budgets and schedules and programs and rules. I wanted to be an instructional leader, but the concept was relatively new, and I had no training. I was figuring it all out on the job as best I could.

These are the school administrators I had known when I took the job as principal of the Parker School. Not a pantheon of role models. It wasn't so much the stress of a *new* job that was killing me—or moving, or building a house, or welcoming our third daughter into the world—it was the job itself and my lack of good training.

CHAPTER 10: REFLECTION QUESTIONS

1. What do you think of a school where all the teachers plan together for several weeks during the summer? Would you sign up to teach there, even if you didn't get extra pay?
2. What do you think of a "retreat" like the one described in this chapter as a way to open each school year?
3. How do you start up a school true to its ideals without running everyone, including the principal, to psychological ruin?
4. What changes in a school when the principal focuses first on teaching and learning and second on budgets, schedules, and management concerns? What does it mean to be an *instructional leader*?

SUGGESTED READING

For ideas on how to facilitate an advisory or a school retreat focused on collaborative problem solving and character development, consider *The Advisory Guide: Designing and Implementing Effective Advisory Programs in Secondary Schools* by Rachel Poliner and Carol Miller Lieber. Another good book is Kris Bordessa's *Team Challenges: 170+ Group Activities to Build Cooperation, Communication, and Creativity.* To learn more about instructional leadership, read *Instructional Leadership: A Research-Based Guide to Learning in Schools* by Anita Woolfolk and Wayne Kolter Hoy. The Parker School has received considerable attention as a model public school. There are two particularly useful books. The first is about the early years that were both hugely promising and distressingly chaotic: *Upstart Startup: Creating and Sustaining a Public Charter School* by James Nehring. The other looks at the school at a later, more mature stage and places it in a context of national school reform. It is Tony Wagner's *The Global Achievement Gap.* Parker is one of three schools profiled as an exemplar for twenty-first-century learning.

ELEVEN

LISTENING AND RELOADING

Nearly everybody involved with the Parker School was against tracking students (honors track, college prep track, vocational track, etc.) because it gives some students an advantage and marginalizes the rest. And on the basis of what? Grades? I.Q.? "Talent"? Flimsy and fuzzy indicators heavily influenced by forces beyond the students' attributes, such as how much money and education his or her parents have and lurking biases in the teaching staff. So all the students at the Parker School were mixed together.

Arts and Humanities classes worked well this way, but there were signs of trouble in math, science, and technology. Some were beginning to question the wisdom of putting everyone together. Were the more advanced students being held back? Were the less advanced students getting lost? Several teachers suggested we create two groupings of students based on their readiness.

The stalwarts, committed to Parker's culture of equity, rejected this view, afraid the school might slip into the comfy norms of conventional schooling, which meant satisfying the vocal parents. A rift was growing. The perceived options were either/or. I was being wooed by both sides, and I did not like the way the issue was being framed, and I did not like being forced to choose. At the same time, I did not know enough about math or science to describe a credible alternative, and I was unsure about how to set up a process that would get me out of the hot seat. I resorted to what I knew how to do: generate ideas.

I brought plans and revised plans and re-revised plans to our leadership team meetings. One day I came to the team with a plan labeled "version 1.3." Donna commented, "Is there a version 1.2? 1.1? Did we discuss them?"

William Isaacs was co-founder in 1990 of the Massachusetts Institute of Technology's Center for Organizational Learning. Early on, the center led a large scale research project involving organizations with intractable disagreements. One site was a steel mill with a deep labor-management rift. Another was a recently merged health care network that lacked a coherent communication system and faced growing discord. The Center for Organizational Learning intervened in these situations and studied the impact of the intervention.

The goal in all three cases was getting people to listen to one another and think together. The challenge was to break through all the cultural and psychological obstacles. This is a challenge that lies further upstream than simply "getting to yes," a popular negotiating strategy that helps people identify their true interests. Individuals, they found, did their thinking in private, and when they came together, they debated their already formed thoughts. Isaacs says this is typical and that in most discussions, "we don't listen, we reload."

I was stuck in the kind of thinking Isaacs writes about. I did my thinking in private. I wasn't listening.

THE ART OF THINKING TOGETHER

Around this time, I was picked as an Annenberg Principal. A group of progressive-minded school leaders from across the country, we met four weekends a year for two years with expert coaches. Funded by the Annenberg Institute for School Reform, our goal was to improve our practice as principals by bringing the dilemmas we faced in the workplace to each other and carefully examine them together.

Unlike most professional development, this was not about acquiring information or learning a new model to "implement." Rather, it was about stopping in our tracks, observing carefully, asking pushy questions, re-thinking our assumptions, and doing so in the company of other principals. I was nervous, but I sensed it was what I needed. Principals, generally, are not in the habit of saying, "I'm facing a dilemma, and I don't know what to do." Much less are they willing to listen, without interrupting, while others question their ideas.

To a weekend meeting at the Doubletree Hotel in Atlanta—they treated us well—I brought a dilemma to my assigned small group of four principal colleagues. I wanted to know whether I should move ahead with a new plan for re-organizing our growing school (version 1.4). Our group was going to follow a discussion protocol. First, I would present my dilemma. Others would ask clarifying questions to make sure they understood the particulars. Then they would ask "probing" questions intended to stimulate new thinking by me. Then, they would discuss my dilemma as they understood it. During the discussion, I had to remain silent. Finally, I would have the opportunity to offer thoughts on what I heard.

I presented my plan swiftly and easily. I was excited about how my new organizational scheme for classes and age levels would solve all kinds of problems. All was well as my group-mates asked clarifying questions. Yes, I had a leadership team with whom I worked. Yes, the school was new, small and growing each year. No, I had not yet shared the plan with the student or parent communities. Then came the probing questions.

"Why did you choose not to include the parents and student communities in the planning discussions?"

"I guess," I thought a moment. Wasn't it obvious? The whole process could spin out of control. Four hundred people planning a school reorganization? No. Much better to have a small group of the people hired to figure out such things and then present the plan to the community for approval.

"I guess, it would seem kind of chaotic to have so many people involved. It might say to the community, we don't know what to do, so we're asking you to do our job." They hired us to run the school, and we were doing our best.

Next question: "So at some point you will present your plan to the community. How do you think they will react?"

"Well, I hope they will like it. It solves a lot of problems. I think most people will be appreciative and breathe a sigh of relief that someone figured this out."

Next question: "If you present it to the community, I guess at a big meeting, and there's some disagreement in the crowd—after all, 400 people is a lot of people—and different people see the problems differently and/or have different ideas about solutions that they voice at the meeting, what will you do?"

"Well, honestly, I guess that personally I'd feel a bit miffed after so much hard work. On the other hand, I know that, as a leader, I need to be patient. So I'd listen and take notes, and I guess we'd say we'll make some revisions based on feedback, though, honestly, I think it's a pretty good plan and if there's a lot of negative feedback, part of me will just want to say, 'okay, you're so smart, you know so much about how the school works, you figure it out!' You know what I mean?"

Next question: "What are the different ways you gathered information on which to base your new organizational plan, and why did you choose those particular ways?"

This was starting to feel like an interrogation. Nobody was asking about the plan itself, and it was a really cool plan. It offered some elegantly simple solutions to a host of problems that everybody had complained about. All the questions were about process.

"My leadership team and I are always gathering information, every day, all day as we interact with students and parents, spend time in classrooms, everything like that. We have a really good sense of what the school needs. We definitely have our pulse on the whole 'big thing' more than anyone else, and I don't say that in an egoistic way. It's just true because of the positions we hold."

Next question: "You said that there are four other people on the leadership team. What role did they play in the development of the plan?"

And so it went, question after bloody question. I was growing impatient, but I felt like I better not show it. I should remain calm because that's what leaders do. We remain calm. If only they understood the school community in which I work, they would get it. I began to feel like maybe they didn't get it. As fine a group of people as they were, they all worked in more conventional schools, not a start-up with all the attendant chaos and uncertainty. It takes nerves of steel. Would any of these people last in my job?

At some point probing questions ended and what began next was even more annoying. For ten minutes, the group talked about my problem as if it was their own, but I was not allowed to talk. I could only listen, "and take notes." This was feeling out of control. The group did not understand my situation and now they were going to talk about it like they were the experts and I would not be allowed to correct them. So they talked and the ideas popped like corn.

"I think Jim needs to open up the process."

"Yeah, it's not about the plan, which I'm sure is a very smart plan with a lot of truly insightful solutions. It's about the story of how such a plan is developed with the whole community."

"Right. It really is an interesting plan and I don't mean to diminish it, but it is not the plan that the community created. It is not the plan even, really, that the leadership team created. It is the plan that Jim created."

"Yeah, and that puts a lot of pressure on Jim!"

At this everyone nodded sympathetically. I was not nodding sympathetically. I was fuming. This whole thing was being twisted into some weird touchy-feely problem. I was being made out to be somehow wrong.

"What if Jim, or perhaps an outside facilitator, were to lead a community meeting in which it was announced that a committee was being formed to look at possible, alternative organizational schemes for the school. You know, something like, as our young school grows, there are growing pains and we want to find out if some of them can be addressed with organizational solutions."

"Yes, and a committee—well, I'd prefer to call it a study group or a task force—would be formed, including faculty, parents, students, and members of the leadership team."

"Right and the outside facilitator might continue to serve in some capacity with the committee or study group."

I could barely contain myself. A facilitator? They were thinking I'm in trouble, that I've lost my leadership mandate or that I don't know how to run a meeting. And a committee? Forming a committee and getting them to understand the issues and develop solutions could take forever. And who knows where they would end up? What if the committee came up with a crazy idea? And what if they were just persuasive enough that the community adopted it?

I finally spoke. "I'm sorry. I know I'm not supposed to talk, but I just have to point out one thing: my school is a very young school. It is facing urgent and pressing issues. We don't have the time or luxury for facilitators and committees and endless meetings. We have to solve problems now. So . . ." I looked around the group seeking acknowledgment. Seeing none, I pressed on. "I think the conversation just needs that information."

Nobody said anything. They all looked at me like they didn't know what to do next.

The facilitator spoke. "Jim, I know it is really hard to hear things without being able to respond. And I appreciate that some of what you are hearing is very hard to listen to. At the same time, for the protocol to do its work, it is very important that the presenter just listen and take notes during this portion of the exercise. Can you do that?"

Can I do that? "Okay, okay," I said, waving my hands.

"I appreciate what Jim is saying about urgency. And it must be very hard to slow down enough to make the process inclusive, but the alternative is to make organizational moves that no one endorses, which will only ratchet up the urgency."

"Frankly, if I were in the community meeting where plan . . ." He paused and looked at my paper where "version 1.4" was printed. "I'd be wondering where is version 1.3 and what was it, and how come I didn't see it, and who decided they didn't like it anymore?"

We turn by degrees. There was painful learning for me in this exercise. There was imperceptible change, like a ship when it changes its heading by a very small amount that is not apparent immediately, yet in a voyage from Lisbon, will land you in Baltimore instead of New York. A life is made up of many such adjustments in course. Each one is small. Sometimes they cancel one another out. Sometimes they cut a path that meanders. And sometimes they produce a gentle arc that over a lifetime leads you to a new destination.

MEDIATING

While I was learning about collaboration, I was also learning about interpersonal relations.

Maureen, our school counselor, told me that if two people are in conflict, usually each person bears some responsibility for the conflict. Maureen also said that much of the time, people in conflict mainly want acknowledgment that they've been heard by the person with whom they are in conflict. When Maureen mediated a conflict, she would say, "Can you please say back to this person what you heard him say?" And then she'd coach the person through the words.

I started practicing these simple, important moves in my mediation among students, and they worked. I started to wonder what it would look like for teacher-student disputes.

Teacher: I asked him to not sharpen his pencil until I was done talking, but he got up in open defiance of my reasonable request, and walked over to the window and sharpened his pencil.

Student: She is such a jerk. I told her when she checked my homework that I didn't get it, and so I didn't do it. And she gets all righteous and says she has some "no excuses" policy and it's 10 points off and that's that, and then she just walks on to the next kid.

In a mediation, the teacher would learn that the student felt wronged not so much because of the 10 points off, but because he was summarily dismissed without any understanding or offer of help. The student would learn that the teacher was angry because when he sharpened his pencil, she was trying to re-teach the material he didn't get the day before. At some point, each person would say how they might handle the situation differently to avoid conflict in the future.

Here's the problem. In most schools, when there's a conflict between a teacher and a student, most of the time—almost all of the time—the teacher is deemed right. It's called "discipline," and schools have discipline policies which identify all the things a student might do to be wrong and what will happen as a consequence. When there is a conflict between a teacher and a student, the teacher often writes a triplicate form called a "discipline referral." The form has check boxes for the kinds of wrong things that a student might do: refused to follow instructions; showed disrespect for teacher; used inappropriate language.

The triplicate form goes to the assistant principal, who then meets with the student to mete out the punishment. Here's what happens: the assistant principal listens to the student and hears her side of the story, and, as he listens he might think, gee, I probably would have used inappropriate language, too. However, the assistant principal cannot acknowledge this because then the student might no longer be entirely or exclusively wrong. So the assistant principal is cornered and must say something weak like, "Next time, handle it differently." If the assistant principal goes back to the teacher to explore more fully what happened and suggests that the *teacher* might handle the situation differently next time, he is violating the unwritten rule that stipulates the teacher is always right. If the assistant principal does this several times, then he is seen as "soft" and "unsupportive," and there may be a grievance filed with the union.

On the other hand—there's always the other hand—schools manage large numbers of students and lack the capacity to mediate every conflict. Policies and triplicate forms streamline the process. What to do? Make the school smaller, more personal. This was a basic premise of the Parker School. It was a basic premise of the Lab School. But changing the scale of the school will not, all by itself, make the difference. The adults who work there need to also change.

COLLISION WITH Z.

One teacher, we'll call her Z., arrived at the door of the Parker School equipped to teach math at a time when we were in desperate need of a math teacher. She had solid credentials. And we *needed* a math teacher.

We hired Z. All was well for a week. Then students began arriving at my office about every other day. We were not a school with detentions or in-school-suspension or three strikes and you're out or "keep-that-up-and-I'll-land-you-out-of-here-so-fast-it-will-make-your-head-spin." We were a school that labored to build relationships, talk through conflict, understand the other person's perspective, respect adult authority, and cultivate student voice. We were a school, as Ted Sizer, our founder, wrote, "that expected much of students, but did not threaten them."

Z. did not get this. Class was about students in rows, no gum chewing, do your homework, and three strikes you're out. For someone committed to such an unambiguous mind-set, any suggestion that "classroom management" is fundamentally about relationship-building, mutual respect, and trust was rejected as "soft." It simply did not compute with Z.

I tried unsuccessfully to penetrate Z's mental defenses. I tried talking with Z. about her students and asking about the situations that resulted in Z. sending a student to my office. All of my efforts were fended off by Z.'s radar which was programmed to read such efforts as *soft administrator*. My greatest folly was to attempt to mediate a conflict that had festered between Z. and a parent. Z. had never met the parent and had communicated with the parent entirely via email.

The student in question was not one who Z. had sent to my office. The student was, in fact, a model student by almost anyone's standard, but what was problematic for Z. is that this student had a voice and used it to express her growing concern about the classroom culture that Z. was cultivating. The tension this caused bubbled over into a classroom confrontation in which the student was "insubordinate," a term used by Z. to describe what had happened. Interestingly, this is a word frequently used on triplicate discipline forms. The email conversation between Z.

and the parent moved into high gear, and then there was a phone conversation, a positive step for communication. However, not surprisingly, the
phone conversation did not go well. This is when the parent called me.

I set up a meeting between Z. and the parent with me in my office. At
the meeting, I tried my best to be Maureen-like in my mediation. Z.
owned up to some missteps, the parent offered understanding comments
about the challenges of teaching teenagers, and it appeared that we were
starting a new chapter. Until several days later, when I learned via the
grapevine that Z. had been talking to other teachers all about the "am-
bush" I had arranged for her and how I was completely unsupportive
and soft as a principal. This was one of several moments when the bow of
my career ship turned a couple degrees away from its intended course of
happy, life-long school principal.

Perhaps I should have intervened sooner. I could have spent more
time in Z.'s classroom. I could have enlisted the domain leader to work
with Z. I could have been clearer during the interview with Z. about the
culture of our school and how we manage relationships. I could have
provided support in meeting our standards, and I could have made clear
my expectation that she meet those standards. But I did none of these
things, partly because the school's standards with respect to student culture at this early phase were still murky, partly because the mountain of
work on my desk was so high, and partly because I wasn't clear what it
meant to be an instructional leader. And partly—perhaps most impor-
tantly—I did not want to be responsible for other peoples' bad teaching.

A seasoned principal of a school similar to Parker whom I spoke with
around this time told me when I said I missed teaching that I had to see
my teachers as my students and my faculty meetings as my classroom. I
replied that I had a hard time doing this because I wasn't their *teacher*, I
was their *leader*. What I did not fully appreciate is that, for some, I had to
be both.

YOU CAN'T MAKE ME

Around this time, I began to worry that our school was drifting back-
wards into the cold embrace of "discipline." I noticed one day that the
towel dispenser in the boys bathroom downstairs was bashed in. One or
more persons had taken a fist to it. Since it was made of metal, you'd
have to whack it pretty hard to bend it out of shape. You'd have to be
pretty angry. Soon we went to a system of students requesting a key to
the bathroom in order to use it. I hated that.

Meanwhile, in the girls bathroom, it came to the attention of our
school counselor that certain girls were stopping in for a "nip of something" in the morning. There was also a rash of thefts. A small CD player
had gone missing in one classroom. A wallet disappeared and reap-

peared the next day without the $40 that had been in it. A young man, whom I suspended for threatening several students, put his fist through the wall on his way out of my office. A fight between two boys broke out in the parking lot after school one day. Another fight broke out between two girls in the parking lot after school on another day. This fight was part of a feud between rival girl groups which, as I contacted homes, appeared to extend to several sets of parents.

In response, I counseled, mediated, investigated, referred, invoked the student justice committee, suspended, cried, and went home exhausted. I started the day exhausted just thinking about it all. I met with teachers and parents to try to understand what was happening. Was this normal? Did we, as a school, have a problem?

One day it came to my attention that a group of students wanted to meet with me about the question of school discipline. I agreed to meet, and it turned out that their visit was prompted by my recent suspension of one of their friends, a matter I could not discuss with them. Nonetheless, I agreed to listen to their concerns. We spent a lunch period together in an unsatisfactory conversation in which I mostly listened.

One day we had a fire drill. The whole school exited the building in a relatively speedy and organized fashion. Walking around the outside, I noticed a clot of students near one of the rear exit doors and remembered the fire chief telling me not long ago that all entrances and exits needed to be free for fire personnel. I walked over. A dozen students were chatting benignly while they waited for the signal to re-enter the building. I got to the edge of the group, and, to get their attention, called to Randy Talty, who I saw standing nearest to the door.

"Hey, Randy," I called. "You guys need to move away from the door."

"Why?" asked Randy.

"Because it's a fire drill, and we need to keep the doors clear." I thought it mildly inappropriate being questioned during a fire drill, but it was a question, so I answered it.

"But if someone needs to get in or out, they can. So why do we have to move?" Randy replied casually. No one moved. Randy seemed to be crossing a line.

"Randy," I said in a tone of tried patience, "The fire chief told me we have to keep these doors completely free of people. Please step out onto the lawn."

I guess my "please step out onto the lawn" sounded too much to Randy like "please step out of the vehicle." I was, in this moment, the Cop.

"You can't make me," Randy muttered, and before my vocal chords could respond to the rising blood pressure in my ears, he and the others began to slowly move away from the door.

"Thank you," I said with strained evenness, under which surged mighty currents of pressure. I turned and continued on my tour.

Somehow, the spirit of inquiry we sought to cultivate in our pioneering, progressive school was turning, for some of our adolescents, to a spirit of petulance. And I, in my effort to call out the petulance, was gaining a reputation as the Cop.

This was ironic. In all of my previous incarnations, I was anything but the Cop. I always sought ways to manage large numbers of students that were not oppositional, and I generally succeeded. In my classroom, I could successfully lead a reluctant, distracted mix of students with engaging activities and a lot of relationship building in the background. As the principal, I did not design engaging activities. It was no longer my job. And it was difficult to build relationships with students when I did not interact with them daily in the classroom.

I felt that my two chief tools for effective group management had been taken away, while the size of the group I was expected to manage—the whole school—had grown exponentially. As a teacher, I thrived on the close relationships I built with my students. As a principal, I was starving, and without a solid relational foundation, I felt increasingly like a fraudulent adult in their midst, an adult whom they could dismiss.

A CULTURE OF "YEAH, BUT . . ."

Around the same time, faculty meetings began to change: I start the meeting. "So today, we're going to review the schedule we've been using for the last month. To do this, we're going to first divide into several groups of about five people each. Each group should include a range of perspectives—by domain, by division. Once you are in your group, you will take time to consider what is working about this schedule and what is not working. Make a list for each of these two parts of the discussion. We'll then reassemble as a group and share out. This is the first step in a multi-step process, the goal of which is to ensure that we are using a schedule plan that offers us the most for the priorities we set. Is our schedule basically working and it needs only some refining? Do we need to consider starting over? Does this make sense? Are there any questions before we begin?"

Silence. I wait three beats. I start an uptake of breath in advance of saying something like, "Very well then, form your groups and let's begin." But before I say that, a hand goes up. It is Raymond.

"I just . . ." Raymond begins. Some people who are already part way out of their seats to form their groups freeze. "I think maybe there's a deeper question that we need to consider first."

Raymond states his deeper question. "What are the priorities that we are trying to manage with our schedule? I mean, how will we know when the schedule we have is the right schedule?"

I am unprepared for the deeper question. I don't know what to do. Others pick up on the deeper question theme. There is some discussion. Other issues are raised.

"How come the wellness program is always the handmaiden of everything else? It feels like we exist in order to open up planning time for the other teachers."

"Are we meeting the state requirement for instructional hours? Do we know what the requirement is?"

"Our Spanish program needs more time in the schedule, but it always gets pushed to the bottom of the list."

"Does advisory count as instruction?"

We do not move into our groups. We talk all together for about forty-five minutes. A dozen unresolved issues are brought to the table. I conclude the meeting saying that the leadership team will consider these issues. We disband.

A feeling of defeat fills the room. What I did not understand at the time is that our young staff was anxious. They needed reassurance. A few well-crafted calming remarks might have bridged the difficult moment and gotten us into the planned agenda with all their questions still in the hopper. But I didn't get that, and I didn't know how to do it. I was exhausted. I didn't want to be the teacher. Truth is, I didn't want to be the leader.

I walked back to my office. My mind was drifting. I thought about the abandoned shopping plaza on my way to work, where a truck driving school operates. Sometimes, on my way home from school in the late afternoon, I'd see maybe ten trucks driving in a line through a course marked with pylons, or I'd see the trucks parked side by side, and standing nearby, a huddle of student drivers with their instructor. They looked eager, and they ranged from kids to retirees.

I could be a truck driver. I could take a class and get a special license. I could get steady work. And then I could take off for weeks at a time, drive long, lonesome highways out west. I could ride hundreds of miles at a stretch on a straight road that just keeps disappearing over the horizon. I could listen to music and radio shows, and then stop for food. Breakfast would taste great after several hours of early morning driving. I could sleep in the truck since trucks have sleeping compartments with a bed and a TV and pretty much everything you need. The goal would be crystal clear: haul stuff from point A to point B. It would be like digging a ditch.

CHAPTER 11: REFLECTION QUESTIONS

1. When do you find yourself listening in the way Isaacs means it? When do you find yourself re-loading? Are you accustomed to

thinking privately and debating with others, or thinking together and constructing new insights? How are these two modes different from one another? How do the outcomes differ?

2. Why is the process for making an organizational decision at least as important as the decision itself?

3. The discussion protocol in this chapter is a painful experience. Why is it painful? What is the learning that comes from it? Why is the protocol so powerful? Have you experienced protocols like this? Can you think of ways a protocol like this might be used in your own work?

4. What are the differences between mediation and "discipline" as described in this chapter? Are there times when each is called for? How do you decide?

5. How do you manage conflict in ways that promote learning? How does a school cultivate a tone of decency?

6. Must a school be small in order to foster a tone of decency, a culture of mediation, shared respect?

7. Is it inevitable for your relationships with students to attenuate as you move up the ranks of school leadership?

SUGGESTED READING

For an exploration of the generative nature of authentic dialogue, read William Isaacs' *Dialogue: The Art of Thinking Together*. An excellent handbook on protocols is Joseph McDonald's *The Power of Protocols*. The classic treatise on the merits of small organizations is *Small Is Beautiful: Economics as If People Mattered* by E. F. Schumacher.

TWELVE

SIX MONTHS LATER

"Tide's up," says Trish, my teaching partner, breezing past me in the faculty room. It's 8 a.m., and I've just arrived at school. It rained all night. "The back two rows are under water," she adds, gathering papers from her desk. Five minutes later, I walk into our basement classroom. Sure enough, water has seeped through the exterior wall at the back of our room, and the floor is awash in about an inch of floodwater.

Water has engulfed the two back rows and is advancing toward the third. Fortunately, our classroom is wide, which means we can take chairs from the back and add them to the side so no one has to put on waders. Whenever there's a lot of rain, the room floods. It's never taken over the whole room. We've never been actually displaced. To some it is annoying, to others amusing. For me, it is just the kind of absurdity that makes me happy to be a teacher.

Somewhere around December of my second year as principal teacher of the Parker School, I began to feel permanently exhausted by the job. The mountain of work that during the first year seemed, with very long hours and continuous preoccupation, sometimes manageable, was now out of control. The school had doubled in size, and we were building a budget and program for the coming year when it would be nearly triple. In addition to carrying out my principal functions, I was teaching Spanish. When a teacher suddenly left in the late winter months, I assumed half of her teaching load. All the big discipline cases continued to come to me.

We surveyed the faculty to see how things were going. The message that came back was clear: we need more support from the top. Our part-time principal, part-time teacher plan was not working. The principal job had to be expanded to full time. Staying in the job would mean a clear shift away from teaching into full-time managerial work.

Laurie and I pondered our options, which included a return to my former job in Albany, where my on-leave status was still active. By strange chance, our old house was for sale. Another option, however, was to stay at Parker as a full-time teacher. I explored this possibility with the trustees, including Ted and Nancy Sizer. Ted and Nancy had become informal mentors through my tumultuous principalship.

Given the time of year (April), it would be difficult to find a really good new principal to replace me. This is when Ted suggested over lunch one day at Tiny's Family Restaurant that perhaps an experienced, retired school principal living in the area might be available to serve on an interim basis for a year while we conducted a search for a permanent principal. I did not at first realize what he was intimating. With further tactful prompting from him, I finally got it.

"What about you?" I asked Ted.

We quickly put all the pieces into place. I would quit as principal to become a teacher in the arts and humanities domain with a reduced salary. Ted and Nancy would serve pro bono as acting co-principals for one year. The trustees endorsed the idea, and in a whirl it was done. I was out as principal and in as a teacher.

Complex matters can often be reduced to a few simple words that are at once an oversimplification and a path to a signal truth. To wit, teaching kids is more fun than kicking them out of school. The principalship, though driven by various responsibilities, regularly returned to difficult disciplinary cases, usually cases that had already pushed beyond several efforts at mediation or sanction—which failed each time—and had some combination of students, teachers, and parents snarling at one another over what seemed an intractable problem. The principal was called on to "fix it."

In a school where the adults genuinely like kids and regularly develop close bonds, the process of suspending a student is especially painful. A steady diet of discipline and suspension is taxing, to say the least. My delight, therefore, in moving full time to the classroom was great. I was rediscovering teaching, and rediscovering it in a place alive with the principles I embraced.

A DREAM COMING TRUE

In all three divisions at the Parker School, near the end of each semester, there is a time when responsibility for the work shifts from teacher to student. It never rests solely on the teacher's shoulders since the work is defined by projects that students are continuously at work on. However, near the end of the semester, the focus turns from individual projects to the preparation of a portfolio representing anywhere from a semester to two years of work.

In a school where the metaphor of student-as-worker and teacher-as-coach is taken seriously, student agency, at this point in the semester, becomes radicalized to a degree that can take your breath away. There is very little whole class instruction. There's no longer a need to plan lessons per se, or design curriculum for the next unit. It's all about coaching students through the work they know they need to do.

For a teacher untutored in the ways of the school, it would be a completely unnerving experience as there would be "nothing to do," meaning the absence of any traditional norms. Students do not appear at the beginning of the hour seated in their columns and rows with shining faces pointed toward the front of the room awaiting the first instruction of the day. Instead, they show up, each with their own tasks that they must define and carry out. Their teacher can help them individually, but there is very little to be said to everyone together.

Ceding control to individual students under these circumstances requires an understanding that the work of the student in that moment is to manage his or her own priorities and that the job of the teacher is to help the student do that. In a conventional school, the teacher manages the priorities of the whole class by structuring activities in service of an objective. During this time, at this school, the teacher's role as the engineer of whole class activities largely vanishes. And yet the teacher must still manage the class. This is the unnerving part.

I grew to love this time of the semester because I believe it was just what Ted Sizer imagined when he said student-as-worker, teacher-as-coach, as happens in sports. If a track and field athlete is training for the 400-meter race, she knows what she wants to accomplish, and she's driven to achieve. It's her desire that drives the work. At the end of the semester, many of the students are getting ready for their gateway exhibition. They know what they need to accomplish, and they are driven to achieve. Like the runner, they will perform in front of others on a certain date. They want to be ready.

The work I was doing as a teacher at the Parker School during this period was a realization of much of what I'd barely been able to imagine when I started at the Middle Valley Middle School. Back then, I'd wondered what it might be like if teaching were more like coaching track. That is exactly what I was now doing. Back then, I'd wistfully imagined the positive difference I could make if I knew my students as individuals and not just as the squirrely kid in the second row, third period. Now, I saw my students in advisory and class, and I taught far fewer students than I had at Middle Valley.

My work was, in many ways, a dream coming true. I began to understand adolescence differently. I began to understand human potential differently.

GROWING INTO YOUR OWN TRUE SELF

It's June and the Parker School Commencement Ceremony has just concluded. The gymnasium is decorated for a reception. There are fresh garden flowers everywhere. Many of the guests are alums, and some among them are my former students.

I'm talking with Robert. He is now twenty-six years old and works in sales for a startup company. It is his second startup company. He was very successful with the first one, but when it got sold to a bigger company, the bigger company came in with their procedural manuals and Robert got bored. He left, and now he's with another startup where he gets to apply his unique talents.

I taught Robert when he was fourteen, and he exhibited the classic symptoms of attention deficit hyperactivity disorder. He was impulsive and inattentive, not so unlike other little boys in my classroom and occasionally some girls. Robert was just a bit more so. He is by all appearances and accounts a successful and happy adult.

I run into Tony, another alum. When I knew Tony in my high school classes he was a sweet, very bright, highly disorganized, verbally impulsive adolescent. We talk. He presents as a mature, energetic, polite, socially adept adult. He is an elementary school teacher and speaks of his work as a calling.

When our dog was a puppy, he had oversized paws. He looked funny and he was a bit clumsy. He grew through it. When we see young people in high school, we're seeing them in their oversized-paws-clumsy stage. They grow through it.

What children need, adolescents especially, from the adults around them, is a safe, well-padded space in which to thrash about. Everybody has traits. They're all different. We're all different. We can sand down the sharp edges, prune the gangly branches, or we can let people be and concentrate on helping them grow into their own true selves.

I composed music when I was in high school, an audacious act given my ignorance of music theory or composition. I composed a choral work based on the biblical Psalm 150. I composed a twelve-tone piece for an instrumental sextet and wrote songs for piano and voice. I hadn't taken piano lessons, but nobody told me I couldn't do this, so I did it.

Actually, that's not true. My older brothers, who tried to sleep in on Saturday morning, told me to stop in clear, unambiguous language when I was pounding out melodies and chords on the piano in the living room. My mother told me to play more quietly. Then she told my brothers to leave me alone because I was experimenting. That then became the brotherly taunt for anything annoying that I took on. Jimmy was "experimenting."

But isn't that what you do as an adolescent, experiment? We should give our teenagers safe space to do it more. Maybe that is what the Parker School does best.

CAFÉ WEDNESDAY

Café Wednesday is a more or less monthly performance venue at the Parker School for students who want to get up in front of their peers to sing, act, tell jokes, mime, dance, play the piano, perform magic, read their own poetry, read other peoples' poetry, show slides, or tell stories. There are no auditions. Students just sign up. There is light oversight to ensure acts are appropriate.

I'm attending one evening. First up is Jillian. Jillian sings a popular song from the radio with gusto. She moves around the stage, working hard, if somewhat stiffly, to establish presence. She hits some great notes, misses a few, looks embarrassed, recovers, keeps on singing, keeps on moving. She finishes and the crowd claps enthusiastically. There are hoots and whistles. Jillian heaves a deep breath of relief, bows lightly to her audience, and exits the stage.

After the applause has died down and before introducing the next act, Sam, the student MC, says, "That was great! Please give it up again for Jillian!" Mighty applause erupts, more hoots, more whistles. Jillian, who is seated, is talking excitedly with her friends.

Next up is Rob, who will tell jokes, according to the program. His arms hang at his sides as he stands at the microphone.

"Good evening," he says slowly in a deep voice with his lips touching the microphone, making a background scratchy noise.

"Have you ever wondered why you can pick your ear, but you can't pick your nose?" he asks flatly. He then waits, moving his face into a look of wonderment, then after two beats, changes his face to a slightly different scrunched-up look. His timing is good, and the joke, which got the audience's attention, gets a boost from his follow-up antics. Rob acknowledges applause without breaking character by tipping his head, turning, and walking off slowly, eyes straight ahead. This elicits more laughter, more applause, more hooting.

Later in the show a band comes on. Two electric guitars, a bass, and a drum set. A retro punk sound pushes back the walls, vibrates the back of my chair and the floor under my shoes. The song has one chord with fast strumming and a fair amount of shouting into the mics by the two guitarists. Five minutes later, they conclude with a cascade of massively distorted guitar licks, a brutal workout involving every piece of the drum set, with bass guitar notes sliding wildly up and down the neck of the instrument. The crowd goes wild.

The unspoken rule of Café Wednesday is you clap for everyone—enthusiastically. Clap for their willingness to try something in front of a live audience. If it's their first time, clap to honor their first time. If they are really good, clap because they are really good. If they falter, sing out of tune, drop a line, trip, appear nervous, appear *very* nervous, then you clap even more to show your support.

I attended a Café Wednesday once where I sat near an adult who was, at the time, a new front office volunteer. She was a parent from one of the more expensive zip codes from which the school draws. I am certain that at the high school in her hometown, a "talent show" would be carefully vetted, competitively auditioned, thoroughly rehearsed, and presented with the expectation that it better be really polished because this is, after all, so-and-so township.

At that school, the audience would be critical judges. Applause would be polite for the okay acts and appropriately loud for excellent acts. There would not be a standing ovation for anything. This is only high school, after all.

I remember watching her reaction to a girl who sang as a true beginner, faltered mightily, nearly cried, but finished her song. The crowd—as is customary in such circumstances—went wild. The front office volunteer seated next to me puckered up her face with a look of deep incredulity. Later the same evening, a young man with a guitar was strumming quite nicely, but voicing somewhat off pitch. The audience was taking it in stride. No side glances, no snickering. All pure, appreciative support.

The woman, though, I could tell, was completely beside herself. Why, she must have been thinking, is no one else showing any sign that there is something wrong here? Are they all musical idiots that they don't realize every other note is off? She looked from side to side, seeking confirmation in the face of anyone. Everybody just smiled and looked on winningly.

I had a conversation with a colleague in the early days of the Parker School about "strengths and weaknesses." She was losing faith in this conventional construct for evaluations, whether evaluations of young people in schools or adult workers. Does anyone ever really "work" on their weaknesses, she asked?

Our conversation was prompted by PLP season at school. The PLP, which stands for Personal Learning Plan, was a document that was crafted each year for and with each student outlining learning goals. Typically, it included a list of the student's "areas of strength" and "areas of weakness." Sometimes the latter was couched in softer language, "areas for continuing focus." What if, she said, we articulated our strengths, all of them, and just worked on those? Wouldn't that be enough?

UNNATURAL BEHAVIOR

A classroom is a pretty restrictive space in which "normal" can occupy only a narrow band of behavior. As a student, most of the time they're being asked to sit in a chair at a desk for hours, with a few minutes to stretch and change classrooms once an hour. For many, this is unnatural behavior. It seems quite likely that many students under such conditions would buckle and wiggle too much, talk too much, get up and walk around the room, get angry and challenge the teacher or poke at their classmates.

If a student does this chronically, we say he has a disorder—such as attention deficit disorder—and the student is prescribed powerful medicine to still the wiggling and the talking. When this is accomplished, we declare victory over disease.

"Normal" just means what is acceptable under certain circumstances. Somebody decides what is acceptable and that becomes normal. Anyone who strays becomes abnormal. I estimate there is a small percentage of children for whom this is an acceptable idea. In the weird, unfriendly environment we have constructed called school, such children thrive. They become high achievers. The rest of the students learn over time that they are not so special or gifted or that, in fact, they have problems. They have a "disorder." When the bar for order is set very high, the possibilities for disorder expand accordingly.

STANDARDIZED CHILDREN

The same law that established charter schools in Massachusetts in 1993 also established a test. It was to be a standardized test that all students in Massachusetts would take. This was called accountability, a response by angry policy makers to what they saw as foot-dragging, self-protective teacher unions that were failing to produce results in the state's public schools. The test was a weapon created by one group of adults to be used against another group of adults, and the state's children served as handy cannon fodder.

During the time I was teaching at Parker, a protest movement was growing in response to this test. The test forced teachers to focus on memorization of facts. While some things deserve to be memorized—times tables, the ten most recent presidents—it is just one small part of a good education. The test was a threat to intellectual growth and social-emotional learning so powerfully in evidence at the Parker School.

In the year 2000, the test became a graduation requirement for every student across the entire state, and I could stand it no more. After twenty years of teaching, I'd found a school that got it right, and now politics was going to ruin it.

The test was actually four tests: math, English, science, and social studies. The social studies test consisted of multiple choice items and a few "open response" questions that asked for memorized answers from a state curriculum 200 pages thick that teachers were expected to teach. Teaching the entire curriculum meant pouring a dumpster load of facts into every class without discussing the possible meaning underneath any of them.

It was educational malpractice, and I wasn't going to do it. Administering the test felt like serving as accessory to a crime.

I met with my principal and asked him if I would lose my job if I chose to not administer that particular exam and was absent from school on that day as a matter of conscience. Thankfully, he said no. I was grateful. I decided to return the portion of my salary representing that day's work to the business office. But then the question was, what should I do on my not-so-cheap day off?

I thought about writing letters to my elected officials pleading that they eliminate the MCAS. Then I thought, if I'm going to forfeit a full day's pay and face who knows what kind of reaction from colleagues, students, and parents, I ought to get a bigger bang for my buck. Should I put on a demonstration maybe? What if I demonstrated in front of the State House? What if I somehow got people walking by to look at the test itself and let them judge its merit?

It occurred to me that the entire test from the previous year, always kept very secure before it is administered and delivered to schools all across Massachusetts, was now "de-classified" and available online. I downloaded, printed, and cut it up. What if I set up a sidewalk stand in front of the State House and invited passersby to take an MCAS quiz consisting of a few items clipped from last year's exam? What if I sent a letter to every member of the Massachusetts legislature inviting them all to step out of the office for a few minutes that day and take the quiz? This is when a friend and co-teacher decided to join me.

Daniel suggested we give a piece of candy to anyone who scored 100 percent on the quiz and a "NO MCAS" button to anyone who failed. He bought the candy, and I ordered the buttons and posted letters to legislators. Then we decided to invite the press. We wrote a press release that described how we would forfeit a day's pay to administer our own MCAS quiz to passersby as well as invited members of the state legislature on the steps of the state capitol. We sent it to fifty newspapers and TV and radio stations. Then we waited.

As the appointed day approached, a few polite inquiries from the press came in. From our legislators, there was conspicuous silence. May 25, the day of the exam, dawned sunny and warm. We hopped in the car with all our paraphernalia, which now included a banner that read, "Take the MCAS Quiz. Win a piece of candy!" and we drove into Boston.

Starting a demonstration feels odd. You step up to your location and just start doing whatever you're going to do. When you see a TV report of people demonstrating, the shouting and marching and hoopla is already in full swing, but somebody has to make the first shout, some passerby has to be the first to stop and notice, only you never see a picture of that.

We had a table to set up, a little shade canopy, stacks of literature to lay out, and a banner to hang. As we approached the statehouse steps, we saw a camera crew, then another, then several people with notebooks and tape recorders.

"Are you the guys with the MCAS protest?" asked a middle-aged man with a notebook in one hand and a ballpoint pen in the other.

"We are," said Daniel. I was thinking, we're not *with* the protest—we *are* the protest. If they were expecting a mob, they were going to be disappointed. I started to think we'd already failed.

"Can I speak with you for a minute?" said the man with the notebook.

"Can we get set up first?" said Daniel.

Our sidewalk stand was a roaring success. Press people swamped us all morning. Our quiz was greeted with curiosity. Many people were aghast at the quiz's random and de-contextualized content. The photographers and TV people captured the crowd's wonderfully expressive responses. Interestingly, only one member of the state legislature, a woman representing Cambridge who shared our view of the test, made an appearance.

That evening, we were all over the TV news. The next day, the *Boston Globe* and the *Boston Herald* ran feature stories with pictures. But the best moment came with the eleven o'clock news on the night of our protest. One of the TV reporters who'd interviewed us earlier in the day buttonholed Massachusetts governor Paul Cellucci on his way out of a meeting and asked him if he thought the MCAS tests are good tests. As soon as the governor finished making his standard statement of enthusiastic support, the TV guy pulled a copy of one of our quizzes out of his back pocket and invited the governor to take it. The governor, caught off guard, declined.

The next day several parents met me at the school door:

"Who do you think you are?"

"You're a teacher."

"You're supposed to be a model for our children."

The reception from students was mixed. Several teachers were annoyed that our absence meant fewer proctors available for the test. Others cheered our courage. Meanwhile, the test went forward. Teachers and principals passed it out. Kids took it. Newspapers reported the results. Real estate values rose and fell. Rich kids did well. Poor kids, not so much.

CHEW GUM AND DON'T STAY WITH THE GROUP

Our protest reawakened my interest in civics, and the possibilities for civic education. The following season, Daniel and I designed a ten-week unit that got students to research pending bills. A parent who worked as a lobbyist provided training. We then took a field trip to the statehouse and conducted a lobby day. The students researched bills on issues they chose and about which they cared: marriage equality, open space, higher education funding, standardized testing. Then they descended upon the state Capitol for a host of appointments with their elected officials—something many adults have never done.

While there, we also did the standard statehouse Tour. The tour guide scolded our students in advance, just to be safe, warning them in harsh tones against chewing gum, touching stuff, being noisy, and not staying together. This was completely undeserved as these students, here on business, were serious and interested.

When, in the course of the tour, students asked thoughtful questions, the guide ignored them. Later, marching through the Senate hallways in their best t-shirts, arguing at full volume in the elevators, insisting with clueless schedulers that the appointment was actually for such and such a time, the kids got numerous looks from grownups with suits and buttons and shiny leather shoes. *What are you doing here?* their looks seemed to ask.

Our Lobby Day Unit empowered students in a way that no in-school civics lesson ever could. It also exposed them to a widespread prejudice against teenagers. They had to work to be taken seriously because high school infantilizes adolescents and removes them from the mainstream of adult culture.

There's a bronze bust of John Hancock "First Signer of the Declaration of Independence," smack dab in the main entrance to the statehouse. He penned his signature on the Declaration in enormous letters because he wanted to make sure King George III could read his name. Mr. Hancock offers mute counsel to my students: chew gum, touch everything, don't stay with the group.

CHAPTER 12: REFLECTION QUESTIONS

1. What are we losing as a society by conforming children and adolescents to an ever-narrower band of normal?
2. How, in this chapter, does the Parker School loosen the bands and establish a space for intellectually powerful education? What would it take for more mainstream schools to do likewise?

3. How do you resist misguided policies? How do you actively challenge them? What are the risks? What is the cost of not challenging them?

SUGGESTED READING

For an excellent presentation of the ways in which contemporary schooling kills creativity and pathologizes healthy adolescent behavior, see Sir Ken Robinson's T.E.D. talk entitled *Changing Education Paradigms*, which is available on YouTube. The seminal work on A.D.H.D. by a respected physician is *Driven to Distraction* by Edward Hallowell and John Ratey. For an excellent analysis of the social costs of our nation's infatuation with high stakes tests, read *Collateral Damage: How High Stakes Testing Corrupts America's Schools* by Sharon Nichols and David Berliner.

THIRTEEN

A BACKYARD COOKOUT

It's Friday already and we have no plans. The forecast predicts beautiful weather. We make phone calls to see who is available for a Labor Day cookout.

Ted, Nancy, and Ethan are perched in lawn chairs with drinks. I stand nearby to tend the vegetables and chicken on the grill.

"So, what's the next adventure, James?" says Nancy. She calls me James when she wants to get my attention.

"How about we start another charter school?" I respond casually.

This is something I'd been rolling around in my head as a distant prospect, like maybe in five years, when the girls are a little older.

"You want to start another charter school?" Nancy says.

"Sure. Why not?" Ted says.

Ethan, joining the spirit of devil-may-care camaraderie, says, "I'm in," and laughs, like we aren't totally serious, and he's just playing along.

Nancy, on the other hand, sends Ted a side glance, like she knows from past experience how these little "just-kidding-around" conversations sometimes start rolling downhill picking up mass and speed and all of a sudden you can't stop them.

I explain, "Enrollments at Parker are maxed out and there's still a huge waiting list. And we know the solution is *not* to admit more students. So what if instead we create a sister school."

The next day we were back at work. At lunch, I asked my friend Daniel what he thought about the idea. He was interested, and in the months that followed it was he who took the ball and ran with it. Others provided support.

When the school won its charter from the state, Daniel became its executive director. I served on the board of trustees. The whole time I felt

131

like saying, *it was just an idea.* I didn't think we'd *actually* do it. But all of a sudden, no one was kidding around, and I needed to get on board.

I agreed to serve as chairman for the trustees. The trustees' first job was to assemble a board that was as diverse as the community we sought to invite into the school, but that was also ready to embrace the principles of the school reform organization that was our philosophical home base—Ted Sizer's Coalition of Essential Schools.

I realized in a way I hadn't before that the driving principles represented a liberal progressive school tradition spawned by a white Anglo, well-heeled culture. Our board of trustees was black, white, Hispanic, Arab-American, gay, straight, rich, and poor, Jewish, Christian, well educated and not, employed and unemployed. Would the school reform ideas that the school was based on translate across this range of backgrounds, or were they particular to one slice of American society? They worked at the largely white, middle class, politically liberal Parker School. Would they work here?

Other schools in the Essential Schools network were racially and economically diverse, and very successful, but what it took for such schools to function well made me wonder if I, with my limited experience with diverse groups, had anything to offer.

We decided if our board was going to function, we had to get to know one another, do some real work together, and build trust. In addition to our regular, monthly meetings, we held a series of "retreats," usually on a Saturday morning. We brought in outside facilitators to help us learn what a board does, how to build a mission statement, and how to come to terms with our diversity. We conducted workshops about racism and privilege. We examined our founding principles. We wanted the vision of the school to be alive across the board and across classrooms.

One of our consultants, from a background of white privilege not unlike my own, described himself as a "recovering racist" and said that most white people in our society, if they're honest, will admit that they are imprinted with racism, and that overcoming it is a lifelong project.

Once we'd hammered out a mission statement, I made sure it was printed at the top of every board agenda, and when we wanted guidance for a complicated decision, I referred us all to the top of the page. It was to be our anchor. We were a school that taught students to "think for themselves, care about others, and act on their convictions."

It turned out that money was one of the most challenging topics for our board to work with. Not the money in the budget, but our own money. I woke up one morning to an email from a member of the board informing me of a six-figure gift that her family was going to make to the school. At about the same time, another board member asked me if I could lend him ten dollars. He didn't say what for, I think, because he was just flat out of cash.

The next week, one of our consultants told us that an effective capital campaign begins with the board and how we needed 100 percent participation. We set the bar at five dollars and everyone gave.

I felt the six-figure gift should be recognized. I was about to order a cake for our next board meeting when it was pointed out to me that the monetary gifts of other board members might, from the standpoint and pocketbook of the giver, represent bigger gifts. I ordered the cake, but it was a celebration of the board as a whole for achieving 100 percent participation.

Leading the board represented new learning for me. I find myself most truly as an outsider. It is a source of strength and a big limitation. I've led ably and passionately when the larger narrative was about opposing a force that is some combination of incompetent, misguided, or malicious. That was true for the Lab School and the state's testing mania. It was less true for the Parker School and our new charter school.

Put me in a leadership role that's not about opposing something bad, and I eventually deflate. I had to learn this about myself and I had to figure out how to lead when there's no metaphorical dragon to slay, when the work is simply about building a vision for excellence from the people in the room.

BAD REVIEW

During my tenure as principal of the Parker School, a book that I wrote about the Bethlehem Lab School was published. A review appeared in the Canadian journal *Curriculum Inquiry*. The eminent education historian Larry Cuban wrote it.

Professor Cuban wrote that my book's perspective was "limited and short-sighted," that the author appeared completely unaware of the generations of school reformers before him who had made similar efforts and founded schools and movements with similar aspirations. He implied that if school reformers, including me, were more informed about such efforts, we might be more effective in initiating and sustaining our own school reform undertakings.

At first, I was upset, then I decided he was right. So I went back to graduate school to study the history of progressive education. The good people at the University of Massachusetts Amherst were willing to give me advanced standing for some of the coursework I'd done previously in New York. I drove a little over an hour to Amherst where I was often in class until 10 p.m. Then I drove home.

There's something about driving alone late at night after a day of heady talk. Everything seems solvable. Everything becomes clear. I'm riding route 202 north out of Belchertown, and I'm on a free-association mental jag about progressive schools. I think, progressive schools come and go, but the decidedly unprogressive regularities of conventional schooling endure. Graded classrooms, teacher centered pedagogy, promotion by seat-time, rule-bound cultures, standardized tests, uninspiring curriculum, too much memorization, too little creative problem solving and collaboration.

So all these progressive schools keep popping up just as fast as they get knocked down. It's like there's a vine root just under the soil that sends up shoots. You can cut the shoots off, but the root is still there, ready to send up more. Meanwhile, there's all the creeping Spanish moss—conventional schooling—that wraps itself around all the other plants and strangles them.

I turn off route 202 and accelerate up the on-ramp for route 2, a four-lane highway. No traffic. Open road. I accelerate to seventy.

How do we keep a good progressive school from fading and dying? How do we make such schools more permanent fixtures, more reliably available options compared with the dominant conventional schools? It's as though there have been torchbearers in each generation. Bronson Alcott, whom I've been studying, carried the torch through the early 1800s with the Temple School and other experiments, along with Elizabeth Peabody and the kindergarten movement. In the later 1800s it was people like Francis Parker working in the Quincy, Massachusetts, schools, then Boston, then Chicago. Next came John Dewey and the torch burned brightly through the 1920s and the 1930s. Then the torch was relit in the 1980s with Ted Sizer and the Coalition of Essential Schools and school leaders like Debbie Meier and Dennis Littky.

When I was a teenager, we had a small sailboat. I took lessons and raced on Nantucket Sound during the summer. A sailboat is pushed forward by the wind when the wind is behind you. But, due to the physics of sail and hull, a sailboat can go forward when the wind is blowing perpendicular. More amazing still, it will go even when the wind is blowing just forty-five degrees off of head-on. This means that if you're willing to zig-zag, you can sail, practically speaking, directly into the wind.

This liberating fact comes to mind now as it occurs to me that everyone I've ever admired in education has sailed more-or-less into the wind. I realize suddenly, they did it by zig-zagging.

It's 11:10 p.m., and my mind moves to tomorrow and my classes at Parker. Jeremy owes me his oral presentation outline. Angela's mother was diagnosed last week with liver cancer. I have to read Amy's essay on deforestation in the Amazon.

I pull in the driveway at 11:22 according to my dashboard clock. The big issues of education are still clear in my head, the history is neatly laid out. The mysteries revealed. I ponder writing it all down, but I opt for bed. 5 a.m. and the start of the school day is not long away.

I'm up the next morning, a bit short of a good night's sleep. I stand at the sink and shave. What was I thinking last night? What was the big eureka? Maybe there was none. Just regular thoughts, made big by an overstimulated brain running late on adrenaline, drawn to big thoughts by an open highway, an open sky.

In 2003, I finished my doctor of education degree at the University of Massachusetts Amherst. Laurie organized not one but two parties to celebrate. "Congratulations on this monumental event," many people told me. Honestly, it did not feel monumental. It felt like something I just did, something I plodded my way through the way anyone who needs to get a big job done will just go and do. A little every day and after a while, it gets done.

Truth is, I was tired of thinking about schools and how to make them better and starting new ones and changing the system. I'd spent down all my anger over how misguided the system is, and I'd spent down all my excitement for starting up new exemplars. I fell into a funk.

LIFER

It was the sort of bright June day that makes you squint if you look up. Lawrence and I were eating lunch seated at the front of the school on the low brick wall that rings a raised garden. Students were all over the lawn in front of us.

Lawrence said, "We're thinking about the future and kids, and I need more than just a decent salary. I need to know my salary will grow over time. We need stability."

"Makes sense." I offered.

Lawrence had been at the Parker School as an arts and humanities teacher for three years. He was wildly popular with his students and well liked by the faculty. But teachers at Parker were not unionized, contracts were renewed annually, and our salaries bumped along at the low end of average for public school teachers in the region. Lawrence's wife had given birth in March to their first child, and Lawrence was interviewing for a job as an English teacher at suburban Westown High School, a job he would ultimately take.

"What about you?" Lawrence asked. "Do you see yourself staying at Parker for the long haul?"

"I may be a lifer," I said.

Lawrence didn't say anything, but he turned his head and regarded me. I wonder if he thought about his own future in that moment, and if he would come to a point in his life in which circumstances would dictate a narrower range of options. Rather than choosing, he would settle. I wonder if Lawrence was disappointed with me for settling.

When I was twenty-nine, Damian Krug, a forty-five year old social studies teacher, declared during a casual conversation that he had "just ten years to go." Bob Doyle had said the same exact thing several years before at a different school where I worked. He was forty-five, also.

I was disappointed on both occasions that they were settling. How could you just count down the days for ten whole years? How could you just coast? What does that do to your psyche? What does it do to your weight, alcohol consumption, or students? If all you focus on is getting through, on enduring, your work becomes a kind of forced march.

One day around this time, I said to Laurie in the middle of a long car trip, "Your twenties and your thirties are for having a dream. Your forties and your fifties are for living it."

Laurie said, "Hmm."

Did I really feel I was living my dream? Younger teachers were being offered leadership roles. Tessa was made leader for division one. Paul became an advisory coach. Phil and Lauren were selected as consultants with a school system in New Hampshire that wanted to learn some of the Parker School approaches to teaching.

I rationalized, I'm above all that—been there, done that. But really I was envious and annoyed that I didn't get picked to do exciting things. This, I realized, at some level, is how a person becomes a curmudgeon. People told me I handled the transition from principal to teacher really well. Truth is, I wasn't handling it well. I needed to leave this school and go someplace new, but I didn't know that yet.

CHAPTER 13: REFLECTION QUESTIONS

1. Why do thoughtful, progressive schools like Parker, and similar schools from earlier generations, remain at the margins of public education? What would it take to move them from the margin to the center?
2. Are there ways in which white privilege plays a role in your professional life? Whether you benefit from white privilege or are marginalized by it, are there steps you can take to mitigate its impact in your work environment?
3. Long term experience can lead to growth and expertise. It can also turn you into a curmudgeon. How do you nurture the former and steer clear of the latter?

SUGGESTED READING

For a short and powerful essay about privilege, read Peggy McIntosh's *White Privilege, Male Privilege,* available on the Web. For an examination of the historical reasons that thoughtful, progressive schooling remains at the cultural margins, read *The Practice of School Reform: Lessons from Two Centuries* by James Nehring.

V

Evolve

FOURTEEN

TWENTY-SIX AGAIN

It was a weekday evening in June. Laurie and I were at our computers in the room over the garage, our shared home office.

Laurie said, "Do you know about these two jobs at UMass Lowell?"

"Yes," I said, ever in the know. "They've been posted there for like two years. I don't think they're real jobs."

On the other side of the bookcase, I heard Laurie scrolling the webpage with the roller on her computer mouse. "They look like real jobs. You should apply."

I finished my doctoral degree in May 2003, with a dissertation about the history of progressive education in the United States, and now I was looking—sort of—for a faculty job at a college or university. I got excited about one at the University of Connecticut, but I smothered the chair of the search committee with follow-up letters and didn't get a call back.

I also heard nothing back from Bard College, which was looking for someone to start a Master of Arts in Teaching Program. I was all attitude in that application, telling the search committee what they should and should not do in creating a new program. From this sample of two, I decided, nobody wanted me. The steely resolve I showed in the face of publishing rejection, apparently, did not carry over to college jobs.

More mouse scrolling from Laurie's side of the room. "Really, you should apply."

"What's the link?"

"I'll send it to you."

I wrote a polite and conventional letter of inquiry, accompanied by my résumé and three letters of recommendation. No attitude. No string of follow-ups. And then I forgot about it, consumed with end-of-year portfolios at the Parker School and writing narrative assessments for all of my students. Then, in a burst of *let's-start-summer-right*, we piled into the minivan and headed up to Maine for a week at the beach. Laurie, ever the good model of attentiveness to detail, called home each evening to check the phone's answering machine.

"Rosemary Tomlinson called from UMass Lowell," she told me one evening.

"Really?"

"She said she's very interested in speaking with you."

"That's the person in charge of the search."

"Well, call her up," Laurie said.

I called Rosemary back. Two weeks later, I went in for an interview. There was good chemistry. Within days, I was offered the job. UMass agreed to a January start, with a small stipend during the fall to show up once a week, develop courses, and get to know people.

It was a long goodbye to Parker and a slow hello to my new job, which felt good at both ends. By the time I started full time in Lowell, I felt ready. I knew some people, my courses were more or less planned, and I was starting to think about projects that could lead to articles and a book. I was forty-six years old, and I'd been teaching in schools for twenty-five years. I was in the middle of my adult work life, and I was starting again, not with something totally new, but something in a new context and dimension.

It felt like pioneering land that was partially mapped. I knew how to teach, but could I teach older students? I knew how to manage a project, but was I smart enough to direct a doctoral dissertation? I knew how to write, but could I do research? I was excited by the vast plains of unscheduled time that I could fill—and was expected to fill—with whatever I felt I should study and write about. I had my own office. I could come and go as I pleased. In the blink of an eye, I'd gone from being a very ripe banana, the wizened and curmudgeonly veteran to the "new kid." At forty-six, I suddenly felt like I was twenty-six again.

ROOKIE

Upon starting my new job, I decided I would unashamedly present myself as the new person. Having been the seasoned and comfortable person in one school for a long time, I had seen many new teachers arrive with swagger and pay for it later. Swagger is ease that you have not earned. Swagger pretends an intimacy that does not exist: calling a colleague by a pet name that was bestowed a decade before you arrived. Swagger arrives on the scene, hears the veterans call Robert, the head of the math department, "Ducky," uses it, and gets awkward looks.

The swagger guy sits in a faculty meeting and accentuates his vast experience. "I've worked in many schools, and I know that . . ." Or assumes a knowledge of the school that they do not possess: "There may have been a time here when you could do that, but not anymore." I decided not to swagger. I would embrace my rookie-ness. I said, "May I ask a rookie question?" I sought out the opinions of people who had been around. I listened and held back speaking up (not easy). I erred to the side of formality when greeting new people.

SIX YEARS LATER

Clear December sunlight pours into my office on the fifth floor of O'Leary Library, where the Graduate School of Education holds forth. The walls are decorated. There are framed family photos, my diplomas. There is a quilt with panels made by students and families from the Bethlehem Lab School—a goodbye gift. There are my books, a large oil painting the size of a window, and two smaller ones recently completed by our daughter.

For most of my work life I did not have an office. For a long spell, I occupied a classroom, where the only thing that was really mine was the desk. The room got shared with a hundred-plus students, including some who were not mine who arrived every day for fourth period, and for whom I would politely leave when their teacher—who did not even have his own desk let alone his own classroom—came in to teach one class each day.

There was a stretch of years when I had a desk in a faculty room with about twenty other teachers. Once before, when I was principal, I had an office, but it was more like an operation center with a conference table, planners on the walls, stacks of paper everywhere, and so much bustle I never got around or never felt inspired to decorate it with things like family pictures and diplomas.

Right now there are no visitors. I am reading student essays for my online course, "Dynamics of Curriculum Change." The hall outside my office is quiet. At this time of the semester—classes over, grades due in ten days—faculty mostly do not come to campus. They are home reading and grading student work.

But I like coming to my office to work. I have occupied an office on this hall for six years, but I still revel in the idea of having an office, a place to which I have a unique key, a place with a phone that has its own number, a place where I can work, undisturbed, sometimes for hours on end.

My goal is to read five essays in ninety minutes. I've done three in an hour. "Assess DCC x 5" is what I've written in my list of tasks for the day. DCC is "Dynamics of Curriculum Change." There are twenty-nine students enrolled this semester. It takes fifteen to twenty minutes to read one essay—a relatively short assignment—nine hours to read the entire class. I look at the clock. Two essays to go. I need to hustle up to make my ninety-minute goal. I sip tea and open the file for essay 4.

For twenty-five years I taught school. For most of those years I had 125–50 students. I forced myself to assign at least one major piece of writing each quarter. Coincidentally, it took me about 15–20 minutes per paper. That meant forty to fifty hours of reading each time I gave an assignment to all of my classes. I did not have a private office, and I did not have a schedule that allowed me to set aside three- and four-hour chunks, let alone an entire day to do "desk work."

Earlier this morning, Laurie asked me what my day looked like. I said I was going to have a "crate day." This is our shorthand for when I'll be in my office all day taking care of work at my desk. We have a dog, and when he was a puppy, he had a metal cage in the kitchen, a "crate," as the pet stores call it. "Go to your crate, Luke," we would say. He would obediently head for his cage, lie down, and we'd shut and latch the door. It seemed natural for Laurie and I to start referring to our desks as crates.

I am in my crate happily today, drinking tea and moving through my To-Do list. When I finish the set of essays, I will turn to planning the "Integrative Seminar" for which I have set aside one hour.

The "Integrative Seminar" is a new course I will be teaching in the spring for the brand new Peace and Conflict Studies program that I helped to design and shepherd through the university approval process. I will work, off and on, during the month of January, hammering out the syllabus for this course. Its overall shape is now roughly in my mind.

The challenge, one I relish, will be to articulate the main features—course outcomes, assessments, activities, readings—and then the fine details—criteria for the individual rubrics, specific chapters to be read, prompts for various assignments, project descriptions—so as to produce a harmonious whole from top to bottom, a course that students will find engaging and challenging. That's the goal, anyway.

When I design a new course, I get paid 5,000 dollars. If I consult in a school district, I get between 1,000–2,000 dollars a day. Extra money flows more abundantly in this job than it ever did during my twenty-five year tenure as a high school educator. In a good year, my school district—I worked for three in total—would offer maybe three days of paid curriculum development time during the summer at a rate of 100 to 200 dollars per day.

Consulting was largely out of the question because, like any teacher, I had to be at my own school every day all day, roughly the days of operation for any other school at which I might consult. In order to be seen as a school expert, I have had to leave school, and having left school, I make more money consulting *about* school. When I point out this irony to my university colleagues, they remind me that the vetting process to obtain and keep a faculty job in higher education is considerably more demanding than the expectations for a high school teacher in a public school.

Still, having spent most of my work life in public schools, I feel a loyalty to the legions of smart, serious people who toil under conditions that, for a job that necessarily requires thoughtful reflection to be done well, are heinously oppressive. The institutional pressure is not to do the work well, but to emphasize order, streamlining, and efficiency over learning. Sadly, many teachers succumb, but many do not.

MY NEW SCHOOLING

Maeve gasps and shakes her head at the suggestion. Hal Munson has just reminded everyone at the meeting that at Salem State College professors teach four courses each semester. Maeve, sitting next to me, turns and whispers, "This is unbelievable. When do they do their research?"

I'm looking back at Maeve and nodding, but I'm thinking, *how about five courses all year long, with classes meeting every day, and thirty kids in a class, and the schedule is so tightly packed that you have to plan when you will run to the bathroom? And if you write, you do it at four in the morning.*

Pace is what is most different between the work I did for many years in schools and the work I do now as a professor. Teaching school is go, go, go, every day without exception. Forty-five minute classes, three minutes passing time, students continuously in my face, in the classroom, in the hallway, in the cafeteria, in the front lobby, and in the parking lot. Large numbers of students, auditoriums full of students, hallways crowded with them. And in the rare moments when I am not directly in contact with students, though that could easily change without notice, I face a continuously re-supplying stack of student work that requires care and focus.

If I stop for two or three days, the stack doesn't draw down by itself. In fact, it gets bigger. And, I am required to be at school all day every day, from 7:30 a.m. until 3 p.m. I cannot choose to work at home, run errands, or change my schedule to go to the gym in the afternoon or food shopping. Planning is nearly always on the fly. Confer with my co-workers? That happens mainly over the copy machine or quick-marching down the hall if we happen to be going in the same direction. Sipping tea in a private office with the sun at my back and the prospect of uninterrupted quiet? That is a vision I would not dare to conjure.

On the other hand, in my professor job, I must publish or, as they say, I will perish.

"Jim, your number one priority must be to publish in peer reviewed journals."

Jean, my dean, said this to me during my annual review three years into my job as tenure track assistant professor. It was not until that moment that I fully appreciated how true this was. Up to that point I had yet to publish in a peer reviewed journal. I had been a writer my entire adult life. I had authored five books, one while in my current position, and a score of articles published in a wide range of periodicals. But this, mainly, is not what my current job required.

Articles in peer reviewed journals means research studies, written in a highly formalized manner and published in scholarly periodicals whose editorial process involves review by senior scholars who are enlisted by the editor to read, comment, and pass judgment on the work: accept, reject, or revise-and-resubmit. If it were just a different sort of writing, I could easily master it. I am good at absorbing a style and mimicking it. But this was more than absorbing style. Writing is only the end stage of the main thing, which is *research*, for which there are established methodologies, with which one must become schooled.

I knew something about writing history. But my work was pulling me toward questions that are not answered with archives. I was working with school districts that were undergoing change and the process of change was becoming my subject. I was captivated by a conundrum: in a system characterized by weak schools, a few strong schools exist. We know what they look like, we can describe them and name the traits that make them strong. We are able, sometimes, to create new schools that bear these traits. But we are largely unable to change weak schools into strong schools.

I was working in a district that was attempting such a transformation. The superintendent's approach was to train teachers in scripted programs, hold principals accountable for test results and daily attendance and, at the enormous 3,000-student high school, break it up into several smaller school communities. I was part of a team at the university that was providing assistance to the superintendent.

Parts of his approach I liked—breaking up the high school, building student-teacher relationships. Other parts—scripted curriculum, test scores—not so much. I won a small grant to study the role of the high school principals in this process, part of an effort to get a much larger grant that never materialized. We wanted to understand, from the perspective of twelve principals, what were the opportunities and challenges of the transformation process.

With this project, I began an apprenticeship in qualitative research: how to write a literature review and conceptual framework, how to conduct interviews, how to analyze the data using software designed specifically for qualitative data, and how to write up the study in the way that professional journals want. This was all new. I felt like a beginner. I felt like a fraud. Most people learned this as part of their doctoral training. Somehow, I missed it. But I benefitted from patient and blunt criticism from colleagues who helped me learn.

Then, lo and behold, the paper I wrote from the study of principals was accepted for presentation at the annual meeting of the American Educational Research Association, and, shortly after that, for publication in a major journal. I was learning to speak in a new tongue. Around this time a colleague told me she has a friend who stays, at a job no more than ten years, which, he says is when people start to figure out you're a fraud. I was wondering what my horizon might be.

Stress, for a high school teacher, comes from the sheer volume of work, which issues from the sheer volume of students and frenetic pace of the day, every day. For an assistant professor working toward tenure, the stress issues from the uncertainty of the publication process. Will I be able to produce work of sufficient quality? Will I be able to get it published in the right journals? It is not the stress produced by urgent and overwhelming demands; it is the pressure of having to make it over a high bar.

CHAPTER 14: REFLECTION QUESTIONS

1. Is it true that you're either, as they say, "green and growing" or "ripe and rotting?" Which one are you? How do you know? Are you sure?
2. How do you know when it's time to move on from a job? How do you stay fresh in a job you've held a long time? How do you get stuck in a job? How do you get unstuck?
3. How do you step appropriately into a new job? How do you show the right balance of deference and expertise? What are the risks of erring to one extreme or the other?
4. What does it mean for a schoolteacher to be stripped of even the simple professional dignity of a desk and space, no matter how small, in which to work? Why is this insult allowed so often to take place?
5. Why is it that the working conditions for two jobs focused on teaching and learning—schoolteacher and college professor—are so wildly inequitable?
6. Which is more challenging, the schoolteacher's pace and work volume or the professor's pressure to research and publish?

SUGGESTED READING

Two books about the perils of job burnout in caring professions and ways to manage it are *Burnout: The Cost of Caring* by Christina Maslach and *Banishing Burnout: Six Strategies for Improving Your Relationship with Work* by Michael Leiter and Christina Maslach. For a good read on life in higher education, try Frank Furstenberg's *Behind the Academic Curtain: How to*

Find Success and Happiness with a Ph.D., which offers an insightful look at what it takes to build a successful academic career from choosing a graduate school to navigating tenure and beyond.

FIFTEEN

IT'S OKAY TO ASK A QUESTION

Half of my job was research. The other half was teaching. I was learning a ton about research because it was new, but I was also learning new things about teaching. For example, truths that I had thought applied only to high school extend to higher education, namely, the ways students talk, write, and respond to grade pressure. It should have been no surprise to me since they are logical responses to a misguided system.

Some students, mostly boys, tend to speak in loud, declarative sentences. Others, oftentimes girls, speak in questions. Exceptions abound, but the general pattern I have observed during thirty years in classrooms is confirmed by the research. It is as true for graduate students as it is in middle school.

Schools teach students to state an opinion and support it with reasons. Students write "thesis" papers. One day when one of my daughters was in middle school she was working on her thesis paper at the kitchen table. She was struggling, and she said, "Dad, I'm supposed to write a thesis, but I don't know enough yet to have an opinion." This is a girl who wanted to ask questions, but she was operating in the culture of the five paragraph essay, an entity that exists in schools only: state-your-thesis-in-the-first-paragraph-then-provide-three-arguments-in-three-paragraphs-and-then-write-a-conclusion.

The five paragraph essay rules the American schoolhouse, and its legitimacy is consummated by state exams. In many classrooms, the rule-of-five is further articulated in the structure of the paragraph, in which the student is expected to provide a topic sentence, three "detail" sentences, and a concluding sentence.

It is all about the declarative sentence. Even when we teach "the research paper," we teach students to "state a thesis." It isn't until a student reaches graduate school that we officially endorse question-asking. By then, our students are too well trained.

Conversation with doctoral student:

Me: "Your paper is well written, but I'm not asking you to make a case."

Student: "Umm."

Me: "So, you've taken the topic of the role of the principal in improving the quality of instruction in a school."

Student: "Yes."

Me: "And you offer a thesis at the beginning of your paper that the principal should be the instructional leader for the school."

Student: "Yes."

Me: "Then you provide arguments, backed up with evidence to make the case."

Student: "Right. I guess that's what I've always been taught."

Me: "Right. So here's how I want you to approach this instead. I want you to begin with a question, say, something like this: Based on the findings of empirical research, what effect does the principal have on the quality of instruction? That question will lead you into a bunch of large-scale quantitative studies about effect size."

Student: "Uh huh."

Me: "Next, you could ask, how do principals position themselves relative to the goal of instructional improvement? What strategies do they use? What beliefs do they hold?"

Student: "Okay . . ."

Me: "You'll probably be looking at a number of qualitative studies for those questions. Then, finally, you might ask, are there principal traits positively associated with improvement of instruction at the school level?"

Student: "But if I already know what I think, why would I do that?"

Me: "Let me ask you this, what is the foundation of what you think you know?"

Student: "I've read some articles. I have a lot of experience."

Me: "What did you think before you read the articles?"

Student: "Same as what I think now."

Me: "Right. So the purpose of research is to find out if what we think is actually true."

Student: "The articles I read told me it was true."

Me: "Yes, but is it possible that you went looking for articles that supported your beliefs and left out articles that might challenge them?"

Student: "How else am I supposed to make my case?"

Me: "That's the point. I don't want you to make a case. I want you to ask a question and hold open the possibility that what you think is the answer may, in fact, not be the answer, and you are on a quest to find the answer."

Student: "A quest?"

Me: "Right. You find a range of studies and they tell you different things, and you report all the different things they tell you, and you look for patterns among them, and outliers, and in the end, maybe you can draw some conclusions about what all the studies, as a whole, tell you about your question. And you report that. Those are your findings. What you find may confirm what you think or it may alter what you think a little or maybe a lot. Your research can change you."

Student: "Okay."

Me: "It's about inquiry, not advocacy."

I felt like I was back at Bethlehem High School talking with Rajiv or any of his Model UN buddies.

ANGUISHED ENGLISH

Maybe because we focus so relentlessly on assertions without teaching students to ask a question first, writing for some students remains undeveloped and confused — even in graduate school.

Here is one short example. I made it up, but it's like many examples I've seen. It's from a course I taught to master's level students in our initial teacher licensure program in history.

> *While at the Salem witch trials, Gyles Corey was pressed to death. He wasn't guilty and even though they suffocated him by placing stones on his chest. Then, asking him if he was guilty, he said, "More weight."*

What does a teacher do with this? If I had all the time in the world to really unpack what is wrong with these sentences, here is what I would say.

The phrase with which you begin ("While at the Salem witch trials"), suggests that what is to follow is incidental in a manner similar to the sentence, "While at the market today, I saw Tom Matthews," or instrumental in the development of some developing narrative, as in, "While standing by the roadside, I noticed a shiny coin on the ground." Thus, your opening, "While at the Salem witch trials," might logically be followed by a clause such as, "Abigail kept fear at bay by knitting a sweater." Or, "While at the Salem witch trials, Gyles noticed that the judge walked with a distinct limp." Imagine your reader's surprise then to learn, at the end of a sentence that is set up to be incidental or developmental, that the main character dies gruesomely.

Your second sentence is incomplete, meaning it is an incomplete thought. First you inform us that "He wasn't guilty." So far so good. You've told us something simple and factual and complete, but then you continue by starting a new thought with the phrase "even though." When you start a thought with the phrase "even though," you are setting up a comparison as in "Even though it is only fifteen degrees outside, the children at the bus stop are not wearing coats."

Or, *"Even though I have ten dollars, I cannot buy a movie ticket."* In your *"even though"* sentence, you set up the comparison with *"even though they suffocated him by placing stones on his chest,"* but you don't then provide another element for comparison.

For example, you could have written, *"even though they suffocated him by placing stones on his chest, the witchcraft activity in town did not stop,"* or *"even though they suffocated him by placing stones on his chest, his children continued to make trouble for the town."* On the other hand, it may be that when you wrote *"even though"* you didn't mean to set up a comparison and you just chose the wrong phrase.

Maybe, instead of *"even though"* you meant *"still,"* as in *"He wasn't guilty and, still, they suffocated him by placing stones on his chest."* This sentence works grammatically; however, logically, it raises the question of what *"guilty"* means. When you write, *"He wasn't guilty,"* do you mean, by implication, that you accept the seventeenth century standard of guilt and innocence for witchcraft and, by that standard, you have judged that Gyles Corey was innocent? Or do you mean that the record shows that the court found him to be innocent? If you mean the former, then you are probably the only historian writing in the twenty-first century who accepts the magical worldview of North American colonists of the seventeenth century. If you mean the latter, then you are wrong. The record of the Salem witch trials shows that Giles Corey was found guilty.

Your last sentence is also problematic. *"Then, asking him if he was guilty, he said, 'More weight.'"* When you write, *"Then, asking him if he was guilty,"* you don't name the person or persons who are doing the asking. Is it a judge who is standing next to Mr. Corey while he is being pressed to death? Is it the person laying stones on Mr. Corey's chest? Is it a crowd that has gathered and is chanting? Your reader does not know, and the way this sentence is set up requires that the very next word must name the person or persons doing the asking—that's the rule.

For example, you might write, *"Then, asking him if he was guilty, the judge proceeded to lift up yet another stone from the ground to place upon Mr. Corey's chest. Mr. Corey replied, 'More weight.'"* This change fixes the problem we were just talking about, but a secondary problem in the original sentence still remains. You wrote, *"Then asking him if he was guilty, he said . . ."* Up to this point, this sentence has three pronouns: *"Him," "he,"* and *"he".* It is not clear to whom these pronouns refer.

It appears from the action taking place in the sentence that there is a conversation involving at least two people. One person is asking about guilt and a second person is replying (*"More weight."*) So far in the sentence only one person has been named—Giles Corey—however a whole cast of other characters is implicated since the setting of the Salem witch trials is established in the first sentence. Presumably this cast includes judges, attorneys, townspeople, jailers, a hangman, etc. By making the most recent change to this sentence, the one in which we introduced *"the judge,"* we eliminate one of the three pronouns, but we still have two pronouns remaining (*"Then, asking him if he was guilty . . ."*).

From the context, one can piece together that "him" and "he" both refer to Giles Corey, however, the reader has to pause for just a millisecond to sort that out and such a pause disrupts the flow of the reading and distracts the reader ever so slightly. Therefore, it is probably better to state, "Then, asking Mr. Corey if he was guilty . . ." Now there are plenty of signals in the sentence as to who is doing and saying what. The action is clearly attributed and the dialogue is clearly attributed.

If I had all the time in the world to comment on student writing, this is the sort of note I would need to write in order to lay bare all the issues with the passage as written by the student. Thing is, I don't have all the time in the world, and sometimes I feel like I have all the students in the world.

I can make shorter comments, such as, "ambiguous pronoun reference" and circle the offending words. But the sort of student who is introducing this level of ambiguity with pronoun usage, combined with the several grammatical errors, will likely not be able to sort out on his or her own what "ambiguous pronoun reference" means and how it applies to the passage. This is the enduring dilemma for teachers. It is why the very rich send their children to schools with very small classes so that the teachers can spend enormous amounts of time offering guidance like this. Here's the thing about bad writing— it signals bad thinking.

WHATEVER YOU SAY, PROF

The third pattern that holds across high school and higher ed is the power of grades. There was something gnawing at me that I felt right away in my new professor job. I started to notice it after a couple months. I realized that my very grownup graduate students at work on their masters and doctoral degrees (who ranged from twenty-three to sixty+ years in age) were more deferential than my cheeky Parker School adolescents who called me "Jim." But it was more than the casual egalitarian culture of the Parker School, the one where seventh graders knew Theodore R. Sizer, leading American education scholar of the twentieth century, as "Ted." My Parker School students weren't afraid of me. My grown-up graduate students sometimes were.

I tried to sort this out. It occurred to me that my students in every other school I worked at besides Parker showed a similar deference, so it wasn't something about adolescence, even though "cheeky" and "adolescence" tend to go together. When I collected and then returned the first major student assignment of my professor career, I discovered the reason. It was grades.

I had the power to give grades, which are currency in the academic world, whether it's middle school or graduate school. They accumulate like money in a bank account and serve as capital for later acquisitions. I,

as teacher, solely determine how much of this currency each student
receives.

Here's what deference looks like in a classroom where I offer a deliberately provocative thought about the main character in Steinbeck's *Of
Mice and Men* to my ninth graders in the upper track class back at Middle
Valley Middle School. George has just shot his traveling companion and
only friend in the world of California migrant workers because he, Lenny, who is retarded, is about to be found by a vigilante gang. When he
gets found out, he'll be hanged for rape, and he won't understand what's
happening to him, and it will be cruel and horrible. His friend George
decides to shoot Lenny in the back of the head while he's thinking happy
thoughts.

Me: "So, George is a cold blooded, pre-meditating murderer."
Class: Silence.
Me: (My eyes sweep the classroom as I give a provocative stare.)
Student 1: (Tentatively) "So . . . what do you want us to say?"
Me: "I want you to say what you think about that."
Student 2: "Umm. (Raising hand and talking) Mr. Nehring, you said
he was "cold blooded," right?"
Me: "Yup."
Student 2: "Thank you." (Student writes in his notebook.)
Class: (Everyone writes in their notebooks.)

Now, here's what *absence* of deference looks like.
Me: "So, George is a cold blooded, pre-meditating murderer." (I'm
addressing my division two students—ninth and tenth graders mixed
together—in my arts and humanities class at the Parker School.)
Student 1: "No!"
Me: "Say more."
Student 1: "He's being practical. He's actually showing compassion."
Me: "By shooting his best friend in the world?"
Student 2: "I think he's taking the law into his own hands."
Me: "Is that the right thing for him to do?"
Student 2: "Well, it's complicated."
Student 3: "I don't think anyone has the right to take a life."
In the Parker School there are no grades. Students work until they
meet the standard. Once they meet the standard, they move on.
Sometimes, in a school with grades, there are students who choose not
to trade in the currency of grades. Such students are found often in the
"low level" classes, a category contrived by the system for students it
chooses not to advance.
Me: "So, George is a cold blooded, pre-meditating murderer."
Student 1: "He's a what?"
Me: "Cold blooded. It means heartless and cruel."

Student 2: (In a hopeful voice) "Yeah, it's like when you shoot some-body in cold blood. It's like they aren't defending themselves or shooting you back. They're just standing there and BANG, you shoot them."

Student 1: "That's horrible. That's what George does?"

Student 3: "Yeah, but it's different."

Me: "What's different about it?"

Student 3: "He was his best friend."

Student 1: "You go and shoot your best friend? When you have cold blood?"

Me: "In cold blood."

Student 1: "That's what I said."

So my graduate students are deferential not because they are no long-er adolescents, but because I give out the grades and, by and large, they trade in the grade currency. There are other factors at play—culture, educational background, gender, age—but the common denominator is grades.

Me: "John Dewey by his own account is not a progressive."

Class: (Silent. Writing.)

Student 1: "That is so true. I'm glad that somebody finally said it. Thank you for saying it, Dr. Nehring."

Me: "John Dewey said it in 1938. Actually, though, John Dewey *is* a progressive."

Student 1: "Right!"

At first, I was shocked to recognize so much about teaching in my new environment that was familiar. But almost as fast, I thought to myself, why should any of this shock me? Some students still seem to be know-it-alls after they grow up. Our culture privileges know-it-alls. Bad writing somehow finds its way into graduate school. Grades make people change their behavior. So, why would it be any different? People are people.

My job was to be their teacher. Despite my griping and whining, it was my job to get the know-it-alls to stop and discover the power of a question. It was my job to help turn around the bad writing and the bad thinking behind it. And it was my job to help my students become their true, best, petulant selves despite the persistent power of grades.

CHAPTER 15: REFLECTION QUESTIONS

1. Why does our educational culture value opinions over questions?
2. To what degree are communication and thinking styles gender-based?
3. How do you provide writing feedback that students will take to heart and will actually lead to improvement?

4. Why is it difficult to switch from an assessment system based on seat time to one governed by standards? What would it take to make a change?

SUGGESTED READING

An excellent, practical book about the power of questions is *Teaching for Critical Thinking: Tools and Techniques to Help Students Question their Assumptions* by Stephen Brookfield. For a popular and funny (occasionally in spite of itself) analysis of gender-related communication styles, read the bestselling *Men Are from Mars and Women Are from Venus* by John Gray. For comic relief in the reading of bad student papers, see Richard Lederer's *Anguished English*. A veteran high school teacher, Lederer mines the funniest writing errors he's encountered in a career of reading student work. Lederer has written other similar books, all equally funny.

SIXTEEN

SKILLFUL TEACHING

Good teaching is about the accretion of small moves, nuanced communication, classroom radar, and careful attention to individuals. Good teaching is subtle, and it is best taught through coaching.

Early in my work at the university, I requested and was assigned the job of supervisor to teacher candidates in our initial licensure program. This consists mainly of sitting in the classroom of a student teacher, taking notes and talking after the class is over about what happened. In this role, sometimes I witness teaching that shows skill way beyond that of a novice.

Here is an invented fragment of one experience: I'm in the classroom, sitting off to the side. Tenth grade English with twenty-seven students. The teacher is a young man who is quietly energetic. He isn't bounding around the room. He's concentrating on his students.

9:16 a.m.: Teacher joins one of small groups as it analyzes a poem ("Road Not Taken" by Frost). There's a group of five students with one dominating the conversation. Two appear disengaged. Teacher pauses, standing just outside their conversational circle, and listens/observes. After thirty seconds, Teacher takes a step forward and crouches to eye-level with group.

Teacher: "So how many paths are there?"

Talkative Student: "Two."

Teacher: "Okay, another question—this time I want someone else to answer. In the first stanza, how many paths does the speaker in the poem inspect?"

Student: (Reading) "And looked down one as far as he could to where it bent in the undergrowth."

Teacher: "Good. So he gives the one path a good look. What about the other path?"

Student (Pause.) "He doesn't look at the other path yet."

Teacher: "Right. Now, what's the first line of the very next stanza? Crystal, can you read the first line?"

Crystal: "Then took the other as just as fair. . . ."

Teacher: "Has he inspected that path?"

Student: "No."

Teacher: "But he's taking it—before he's inspected it."

Students: (Silence.)

Teacher: "People say this is a poem about choice. I want you to re-read what actually happens in the poem and talk about how the person in the poem makes his choice. Okay?"

Reviewing the notes I wrote to this teacher, they read:

Everything you did here in this mini-intervention was just right, even how you approached it. First, you stood just outside their conversational space to listen, and you assessed what was going on. Then you stepped closer, signaling your presence in a more participatory way, and you crouched, making yourself, in a physical sense, a group peer.

Then, instead of just offering your thoughts, you asked if you could speak. This simple act of asking permission shows respect for the work of the group, and even if members of the group don't respect their own work, maybe now they will since they see you respecting it. By asking for and receiving permission, you also get their attention. Since they have acted to give permission, they are now poised to listen to you. These are all small, subtle moves that add up in a positive way.

A less thoughtful teacher might have simply barged into the group and asked "how's it going?" Such an entry would have substantially diminished the likelihood that anyone would benefit from the intervention. Also, the focus of your questions was excellent. You clearly had a goal (helping them see, from the language of the poem, the question of choice that the poet is raising).

Also, the sequence of questions was just right. Through a thoughtful ordering, you led them to arrive at an appropriate understanding without your simply telling them. Also, you clearly noticed that one student had been dominating and you drew in other members of the group. Finally, you left them with a task.

I noticed that after you left, they continued to work with a higher level of participation than before your arrival. Overall, this was an example of really, really good teaching!

BEING BLUNT

Sometimes I observe teaching at a much more novice level. Evan (also invented) is a nice-enough young man in his mid-twenties. He needs to amp up his teacher radar. We debrief his lesson.

"When you were talking and addressing the class, you had seventeen students sitting at computer screens. I counted how many students were turned toward you and how many were turned toward their screens.

There were six turned toward you. I couldn't see all of the screens, but the ones I could see had a bunch of different websites going. It would appear that most of the class was not listening to you. That's not okay."

"Uh huh," says Evan.

"Those eleven students missed what you said, and the fact that you did not address it, says to the whole class that listening to you is optional. You're setting up a norm of optional listening. I don't think that's what you want."

"Uh huh. But there's really no way to get them to listen. I mean their computer screen is a lot more interesting than me," Evan says.

"Right." I say. He's got a point. "Okay, when you are talking, have them turn away from the screen. Look, they've got swivel chairs. If you position yourself between the two rows, you can ask them to turn toward you whenever you're addressing the whole class."

"But they'll see right through that," says Evan.

I pause. "Yeah. They will see right through it. Right. So maybe you want to help them see right through it. Be completely transparent and say that you know that looking at websites is a lot more exciting than looking at you, but that the class has work to do and sometimes you just need everyone's full attention. Say that you also know it's difficult to divide attention between the screen and the teacher. Say how you're going to have really clear expectations about individual work time and whole class work time. When there's individual work time, everyone is on their computers. When's there's whole class time, everyone is turned away from the computers, toward the center of the room facing each other. Guide them through it. Tell them you want to see their shining faces."

"Um. . . . Okay. I could try that. That's a good idea."

"And then when you call for everyone's attention, don't start talking until everyone has swiveled around in their chairs and is facing each other and you."

"Okay."

I do class observations for two reasons: to provide guidance and to judge whether the work is passing. Sometimes, I have to be bluntly critical.

I debrief with another student teacher (invented). Matt begins with what he believes went well.

"One thing that went well I think is the whole process-writing thing we are using. It's the Betty Bornstein Method, and we have the posters for the five steps that every writer uses." Matt eyes the glossy posters on the wall. I tense at "every writer."

"Today we were doing step 4: every writer revises." Matt points. I look at the poster. It says, "Every writer revises." It shows a jazzy-looking stick figure snapping a finger under a light bulb that floats in a thought bubble.

Matt continues, "I thought the worksheet worked pretty well because it got everyone on board with how to break down revising. You know, first you read it out loud and write down the three things that sound good and the two things you want to change. And today, because we're working on paragraph four of the five paragraph essay, the students were supposed to state whether they thought their three detail sentences were aligning with their topic sentence." I sit very still. I'm thinking about the question I'll ask Matt to stop him in his tracks.

"Okay, something I'd change . . ." Matt continues, and then pauses to consider the second of my two standard de-briefing questions. "Something I'd change is how, when I was circulating while students were doing the worksheet, I would have checked the homework then to save time instead of doing it at the beginning because that was sort of a time waster because the students weren't really doing anything while I was checking homework."

"Uh huh," I say. "How many students did the homework?"

"What do you mean?"

"I mean, when you checked the homework, how many students did it?"

"I don't know. I'd have to check. That's not my point though."

"Would you mind checking right now, please? Your planner is on your desk."

Matt stiffens at my insistence. He gets up, steps to his desk, consults his planner, and calls back to me, "Okay so nine-ish students either had the homework or had an excuse."

"Matt, how many students did the homework?

Pause. "Four," he says.

"And how many students were there in class today."

"Seventeen."

"Four out of seventeen students had what they needed to successfully continue with the work of today's class."

"Well, homework is a kind of problem at this high school in general."

"Matt, I'm talking about *your* class where *you* are the teacher."

"I've tried giving detentions. It doesn't work with these kids. You have to understand they're pretty hard core," he says.

"Okay, so rather than talking about the group as a whole, let's talk about just one student. Pick one."

Observing someone else's teaching is tricky business. It is made trickier by the unique history of teaching as a profession. Peer-critique of practice has a longstanding place in some professions, but not in teaching.

Architects and artists engage in "critique" sessions in which peers examine and comment on each other's work. In addition, their products are visible and public and therefore subject to all manner of attention and commentary. Trial attorneys conduct mock trials and practice elements of their courtroom work with each other as they prepare a case. Much attorney work is public. Some trials are televised. Physicians do rounds.

Unlike these professions, teaching, historically, has been excruciatingly private, available only to the teacher, his or her students, and, on rare occasion, a supervisor who visits the classroom usually with advance notice. This sort of shrouded practice is protected by the fuzzily invoked tradition of academic freedom (*You, outside observer, may not tell me how to teach*) and the historic absence of accepted standards of practice (*Who is to say that you, outside observer, are right and I am wrong?*) Within this system, whether a teacher learns to teach well or poorly, feels sometimes like a matter of happenstance. These are all matters that have been widely acknowledged in the professional literature going back to *Schoolteacher*, the seminal book by sociologist Dan Lortie and extending to contemporary work by scholars such as Susan Moore Johnson at Harvard University.

Within this system, a college supervisor, that is, a person who is assigned to regularly observe and coach a student teacher, stands at an important leverage point in the process. I will observe a student teacher six times in the course of his semester of student teaching. This is enough to have an influence. The greater influence, however, lies with the teacher on-site, who volunteers to take on the student teacher and under whose daily guidance the student teacher works.

Far more than the university supervisor, this person becomes a model whom the student teacher will emulate. This is the so-called cooperating teacher. During my own student teaching semester, part of my master's degree program many years ago, I was assigned to work with Ken, a social studies teacher at a local high school. I have mentioned him before. He is a major reason that I take my work coaching new teachers very seriously.

THE IDEALIST REALIST

After I was assigned to Ken and before I started my student teaching semester, I traveled to Ken's school to observe him teach for a day. He had several U.S. history classes. The school, like most, tracked students into so-called ability groups. Ken taught two of the "low" level groups. With his seniority he surely could have taught all the honors and advanced placement classes.

The day I visited, he was showing a filmstrip (it was 1981) and struggling for the attention of his students, many of whom were more inclined to look out the window, engage in a side conversation with the student nearby, or put their head down to sleep. Every move Ken made was focused on keeping the maximum number of students meaningfully engaged in the lesson while simultaneously managing numerous classroom details.

When the filmstrip ended, Ken opened up discussion, structured by a worksheet that students were to have completed while watching the film. He called on students, listened appreciatively to their responses, and showed interest while removing the filmstrip from the projector and returning it to its case and rolling the filmstrip machine to a back corner of the room. He knew he could not turn his attention from his students for a moment, and he knew there would be no time later to take care of all the manual tasks with the projector.

In the four minutes between classes, he got ready for the next group. He checked the student handouts that were neatly organized on the counter by the window for each class. He checked his equipment, whether it was the filmstrip projector and screen, or chalk and eraser, or a class set of books to be handed out. And he did this while talking genially with the student who lingered or the early arrival for the next class. He did not appear annoyed or distracted or panicked.

He said to me that first day, "Always make it meaningful." I wondered what he meant.

I took it to mean, don't go the easy route of merely entertaining or filling time. Our work is to help students learn. Therefore, deploy each moment toward that goal.

On our way to the cafeteria later that day during his lunch break, Ken greeted several students, one of whom had him for US History the previous year. Ken greeted him by name and reciprocated the student's enthusiasm. They exchanged some inside joke from last year's class. Then Ken moved on.

During lunch, Ken said there will be days (in my teaching career-to-be) when it feels like I am not accomplishing much, when just holding my students' attention will be a struggle, and that it is on those days especially that I must do what I can to make my students' experiences meaningful, even if in a small way.

Ken meant "meaningful" in a broader sense, as well. As I got to know him, I saw that he positioned himself in his work to maximize his opportunity to make a meaningful impact.

While most senior teachers taught the plum classes—the honors groups, electives, advanced placement—Ken regularly taught several classes filled with high-need students who are also the students most likely to benefit from a skilled teacher.

More broadly still, Ken chose to be a high school teacher, a position he'd held a good twenty years at the time I knew him. During the summer, he taught at Brown University in the master's program, and had he chosen, he certainly could have moved on from high school into a full-time college job, but he was making it meaningful where he was.

To someone who does not understand the work of a teacher, watching a middle-aged man struggle for the attention of adolescents in a classroom might appear comic, or tragic, or just embarrassing or humiliating.

It is all of these, *and* it is important work. This is where society chooses to place adolescents, and while the set-up is deeply flawed, if the adult in the room with them is not highly skilled and committed to "making it meaningful" in whatever small or large ways one can, then the flawed set-up will descend into something far worse. Ken knew it was a flawed set-up—for him as well as his students—and yet he chose to step into it day after day. The classroom was his chosen leverage point for social change.

Ken made it meaningful in a larger way still. He was well educated in his field. He knew the adolescent psychology theory. He knew the social studies methods—sometimes he taught such a methods course to eager graduate students. He had a deep knowledge of U.S. history and cultural anthropology and other subjects. In an ideal setting, with small classes and well-resourced classrooms and loads of teacher planning time, such knowledge might find full expression.

But the reality of American schools is that classes are large, classrooms are not well resourced, and teachers must think strategically just to find time to go to the bathroom. The gulf between professional knowledge and working conditions is a chasm, and it is tempting to chuck the professional knowledge and allow one's behavior to be shaped entirely by one's environment. Big classes? Focus on order and discipline. No planning time? Don't assign writing. Limited resources? Stick to the aging textbook.

Some teachers do just that, and they adopt defensive attitudes about "the ivory tower" and "heady educational theory." Ken somehow avoided that. Against all odds, he integrated his professional knowledge with an imperfect reality. He was an idealist realist.

As I began my teaching career, Ken stayed steadily with me. I don't think I asked, "What would Ken do?" but his persona hovered over every dilemma I faced in my early years of teaching.

In fact, sometimes a picture of him would appear in my mind. He would stand, slightly stooped, in his characteristic way. Somewhat impassive, he would listen, with his round face and thinning head of hair and then, he would ask a question. I didn't have to ask what would Ken do because he was right there asking me what I thought I should do.

MIGRATING ONLINE WITH VIDEO AND AUDIO

Back at UMass Lowell, I'm teaching an online course, and to the same extent that coaching new teachers feels totally natural, teaching online feels completely foreign. I'm nervous and excited about running a chatroom with text, audio, and video. I'm wondering about managing it technically—which buttons to push, where to look on the screen. I'm also wondering about managing it pedagogically: What direction will I give? What purposes will we work toward?

I've led live online chats before, but they've always been strictly text-based. That can be challenging all by itself with twenty-plus students in the "room." One management tool I've discovered is to break the class into groups of five or six. At any one time, only one group may enter text while everyone else "listens."

After a while, I tell the first group to step out and let the next group be the active "talkers." As for pedagogy, I've learned how to lead discussions in the text-only chat universe. I tell my students in advance to arrive with a "Conversation Starter." This could be a dilemma in their teaching practice that is relevant to what we are studying, or it could be a provocative question about a book or article we are reading, or a workplace issue that connects in some way to a topic in the class.

I begin the chat by asking each student to post his or her conversation starter. I pick one, and using our small groups, I lead a conversation based on the chosen starter. But the addition of audio and video significantly raises the bar.

"Hello, Janine, Melissa, Roger, Kimberley, Edward, Stephan, and Sandra."

I'm reading the roster as I see my image appear in the small box at the bottom of the video section of the screen. I look horrible. Apparently, my webcam has a wide angle lens, which has the effect of making my face look pointy and my head balder than it really is. I look like the live action version of a bad driver's license photo.

"Welcome to chat," I say. "Please type something or say something if you can hear me." The message box jumps to life.

"I can hear you."

"Hi."

"Hi, Professor. How are you?"

All six students respond.

"Where are you all located?" I ask.

At that moment my roster box jumps as four more students enter the room.

The audio crackles. "Hi, Professor Nehring. How are you?" A male voice arrives accompanied by a psychedelic visual that appears in the video box. It is swirling yellows, blues, and reds. This is Richard with a not quite working webcam.

Meanwhile the textbox is getting lively again.

"I'm in Boston."

"I'm in New Haven, Connecticut."

"British Columbia."

"I'm in the United Arab Emirates."

Just as I'm thinking that's pretty cool, two more video images appear on screen. There are now three, plus the little box showing my distorted face. I find comfort in the fact that everybody else looks strange. Every other webcam tonight has a fisheye lens, making us all look like we have noses from the same gene pool that produced the Wicked Witch of the West. Plus, everyone's voice sounds like it is coming from somewhere deep in a cave. In the world of film, they call this bad production values. Suddenly in the age of web conferencing, we are all sound and video designers.

When it comes to technology, I am the classic late adopter. As more and more new gadgets and new computer capabilities appear on the market, my late-adopter habit has become more pronounced. I don't dislike technology. It's just that I like the things technology enhances *more*.

I like a good word processing program. I like writing *more*. I like a phone that is convenient and functional. I like talking on it *more*. I like an online teaching platform that is versatile. I like teaching *more*. I therefore wish to minimize the time I need to invest in learning new gadgets and software because it takes away from doing the thing it is designed to enhance.

Unfortunately, because there is a new gadget or new software every six months for some daily activity, I can spend my life permanently distracted from doing the things I want to do because I have to learn the new way to do them. Therefore, in this department, I say teach me as little as possible. What buttons do I need to press? Now go away.

Online courses are convenient for students with busy lives. Most of the work can be done at whatever time suits you—10 p.m. until 3 a.m., if you like. Coursework, outside of chats, is asynchronous. Somebody sends you a message on Sunday morning and you can answer it Monday night. And you don't have to go anywhere. You don't have to drive forty-five minutes to a campus where it's impossible to find parking. You just log on from anywhere.

But what is the cost of convenient? What do you lose? Intimacy, for one thing. You can earn a degree without ever meeting any of your classmates or professors. You'll never sit next to someone, watch how they move through a room, experience the simple, subtle details of face-to-face interaction that we take for granted in our non-virtual lives.

Still, there are benefits besides convenience. The fact that I don't have to respond right away to anyone means I can mull the question, turn it over a dozen times in the course of a day, consider possible responses over lunch and then, that evening, sit down and compose my answer, and maybe revise it before I hit *send*. There's powerful opportunity for reflection with online learning that just keeps on coming at you because you can take your time figuring out what to say.

For my next chat, I have a plan. Cyber chaos will not reign in my virtual classroom. I enter the chatroom at 7:25 p.m. No one is there. I turn on my camera. I key in a note for the message box.

"Hi, everybody! Welcome to chat!"

While I'm writing, a colleague stops by. I am working in my office on campus this evening and the door is open. I explain that I am getting set up for chat and she says, "Put the camera above you. It looks a lot better." I wiggle my externally mounted camera free from where I've anchored it atop my laptop and re-attach it to the top edge of my desktop monitor. But it doesn't make me feel good. It looks like it could fall off at any moment, which, if it happened during a chat could be very bad.

Ping! goes the computer. Jessica has entered the chatroom.

Ping! Melissa has entered the chatroom.

Ping! Anthony has entered the chatroom.

Like magic, right at 7:30 p.m., everybody arrives. All their little avatars pile up in the box on the left side of my screen. All of a sudden, there are twenty-one individuals. I have to scroll down to see everyone.

Next the video box on the right side of my screen gets all jumpy, and at once, three faces appear, looking like hostages in a poorly lit ransom video. I notice that their cameras are below their faces.

I click my *Talk* button on the screen and say, "Hi, everybody. Welcome to chat."

CHAPTER 16: REFLECTION QUESTIONS

1. This chapter suggests that good teaching consists of many, many small, careful teaching moves. Can you think of instances in your own teaching or teachers you have observed where small moves and subtle choices make a difference in overall effectiveness?
2. Why do you think that teaching, in comparison to other professions, is such a private practice? What are the consequences? How do we make it more public?
3. A mentor can be a powerful influence on a young person starting out in a new career. What are the qualities of a good mentor? Have you benefited from a mentor? What's your story? Are there ways you can serve or have served as a mentor to others?
4. How do you act toward a person who is serving as your mentor? How do you find the balance between exercising your own critical judgment and agency, on the one hand, while being open to a mentor's guidance and experience, on the other? What if you don't respect your (assigned) mentor's guidance and judgment? What do you do?
5. Teaching and learning via the web will only continue to expand. What do you see as the strengths and limitations of online learning? What is your experience with online learning? How can we capitalize on its benefits and mitigate its shortfalls?

SUGGESTED READING

For excellent advice from a slew of wonderful mentor teachers, read Robert Fried's *The Passionate Teacher: A Practical Guide.* For insight into the beliefs and attitudes that help generate excellent, in-the-moment, decision making for teachers, read *What Great Teachers Do Differently* by Todd Whitaker. As blended and online learning grows in popularity, there are new books available every month. A good one to help you get started is *Blended: Using Disruptive Innovation to Improve Schools* by Michael Horn, Heather Staker, and Clayton Christensen.

SEVENTEEN

MESSING WITH PEOPLES' BELIEFS

"How about . . . a thousand dollars a day," Carter said. We were on the phone.

"Sure," I said. I almost said, *Wow, that's a lot of money.*

"Good," said Carter. "We'll meet on the 15th to start planning."

With that conversation, my introduction to the world of consulting began. I was to meet with the administrators and selected teachers from Carter's school district, about eighty people in all, for three days during August to help seed work that Carter would then cultivate during the school year.

I knew Carter from my days at the Parker School. A thoughtful educator, he was now the assistant superintendent in a nearby district. He wanted to build teacher collaboration, but also foster a shared vision, take shared responsibility for students, and jointly examine teaching practice so that the school, as a whole, could significantly amp up their impact on students. It made sense intuitively—working as a team, building community—plus there is strong evidence from the research world to support it.

At the same time, it was deeply countercultural. Our three days in August would not be the usual professional development fare of jazzy new "techniques" to try out in your classroom a la Dr. Madison. Nor would it be happy enthusiastic motivational talk in the auditorium. We wanted to mess with peoples' beliefs and attitudes and deeply embedded habits.

"You want me to what?" Ron said.

"I want you to just listen. Take notes if you like, but resist the impulse to respond out loud to anything anyone says."

"Okay."

"This will feel weird, but I'm asking you to just go with the weirdness for now. Afterwards, we'll debrief and you can offer your thoughts about the experience. Okay?"

"Okay."

Ron, a somewhat taciturn and skeptical teacher, was perfect for his role. We sat at seven desks, circled up in a poorly lit classroom on the first floor of the high school in Carter's school district. Ron was being asked to listen without interrupting or responding out loud to five colleagues who would discuss the problem he had put before us.

He had framed his problem as a question, "How do I motivate the unmotivated students in my classroom?" The purpose of the protocol—the same one I struggled with several years before—was to help Ron expand his understanding and gain new insight into a problem he was unable to solve on his own. For it to work, the presenter has to believe *some* of the problems he faces lie within his power to solve, or, at least, manage.

The presenter also has to believe that *how* he teaches plays a role in how his students *learn*. This is a challenge in a profession where teachers often complain of little agency and tend to detach what they do from the impact it has on their students.

Ron dutifully followed the protocol. He surprised everyone by not responding defensively to the comments and questions he heard from his peers. Instead, he became engaged. I understood Ron's discomfort very well, having been in his shoes. He did a lot better than I did during my first time.

The exercises we led during those three days planted a seed that Carter, who was at the time new to the school district, grew in the years that followed into a transformed adult work culture—one in which teachers worked in teams, shared responsibility for student learning, solved problems instead of blaming and kvetching, and enjoyed their work. Recent decades have seen a growing recognition within education of the importance of collaborative problem solving. Not only does it offer better solutions than working alone, it builds shared responsibility for students and a shared vision for the work—both vital elements of an excellent school.

This was my introduction to consulting. Before, I sometimes wondered what it looked like, especially when I heard a professor or a retired administrator talk about it. "I consult on the side," they'd say. I pictured someone in a suit whispering into the superintendent's ear at a school board meeting. But now the mystery was unveiled. And, it turned out I had something to offer. Good consulting is like good teaching. It's mainly about skillful coaching. And people were willing to pay.

BELIEFS FIGHT BACK

"Let me tell you something, Dr. Nehring. I have *no* freedom to do anything. I have my lesson plans checked every day. I have administrators in my room at least twice a week observing my teaching. I have to teach exactly what they tell me, every day."

I'm standing in the hallway of an open concept school. It isn't really a hallway. It's a kind of a lane among the bookcases and boxes and file cabinets that extend about an acre in every direction. I'm getting a tongue lashing from a teacher who is being "professionally developed" by me. We are between sessions in a district where I have been invited to work. Lots of other teachers are milling around nearby, and the encounter seems to be creating a bit of theater made all the more accessible by the absence of walls.

The teacher continues. "So everything you're telling us, it's all nice pie in the sky academic theory. We all heard it in graduate school, but you know what, it has nothing to do with what we have to deal with every day."

Usually, I am deferential when confronted like this. I am, after all, the consultant. I have been hired by the school district to perform a service. I am not the boss. However, at this particular school, I've noticed many teachers are completely uninterested in making any change to their bad situation. Any suggestion is met with "we can't because . . ." filled in with students, or parents, or administrators, or the community, or the department of education. This is a teaching culture which has failed to evolve while its students have changed dramatically from working class, English-speaking, white students to a mix of students with varied cultural and socioeconomic backgrounds.

Meanwhile, demands from above for improved student achievement have been raining down from the state. Everyone is blaming the teachers, and the teachers are blaming everyone else and steadfastly refusing to consider any changes to their own practice. "We're still teaching. They just don't want to learn." It's a scenario played out in many schools across the country: changing student demographics, increased demands from society. Stuck in the middle is an organization with little capacity for change and a professional culture that, at its worst, deflects all criticism.

As I said, usually I am deferential, but on this particular day, at this particular moment, having heard every "yeah, but" excuse imaginable in the last several months of working at this school, I decide to say what is truly on my mind.

"Margaret," I say, after waiting until it appears her verbal storm has died down. "Is there anything else you want to tell me?"

"No," she says.

"May I say something?"

"Sure." She's uneasy. People are watching.

"In my experience, the most powerful people in the world are the ones who figure out how to assert themselves in situations where they have the least opportunity for self-expression."

Margaret shifts and looks around. I continue. "Nelson Mandela spent twenty-seven years in prison, most of it in an eight foot by eight foot cell. But he figured out how to maintain his dignity, how to assert himself as a human being in small ways that mattered to no one but him. Because of this, on the day he was released, he emerged a whole man. I've read accounts of Holocaust survivors who held fast to simple personal rituals to maintain their dignity in the worst of all possible circumstances." I looked Margaret squarely in the eye. "There are many things you do *not* have control over, but there will always be some things you *can* control. Focus on that."

With that, Margaret turned and walked away.

Same school, different day. I've quietly joined one of the many teacher groups occupying classrooms around the school. The group is talking about teacher collaboration based on an article I gave them.

The group is led by Gena, a biology teacher. The discussion is just ending and Gena is leading a debrief. I listen and sense a positive tone. Teachers are thinking about their practice and what lies within their power to improve the learning of their students. The desks at which teachers are seated have been arranged into a circle to facilitate conversation and to underscore the spirit of the work, which is that wisdom flows from the group, not from any single individual. After a few minutes, a man who is seated just a bit back from the circle and who, until now, has been silent, speaks up.

"Mrs. Naugthon." he says. He means Gena. Everyone else has been using her first name.

"Yes, Roger," she says.

"I see that Dr. Nehring has joined us, and I wonder if I might ask him a question if that is all right." *Here it comes,* I think.

Gena says, "Well, we've pretty much concluded our debrief, and we have a few minutes left." She addresses the group as a whole, "Would it be all right if Roger asked Jim a question?" Heads nod.

Roger proceeds. "Dr. Nehring, I began my career in 1975 in Chinatown in Philadelphia. Rough neighborhood. Lots of violent crime. Poverty everywhere. I had five classes each with about thirty-five kids. Half of them spoke broken English. All Chinese Americans. Most of them worked other jobs besides going to school. Some of them supported their families. They had rough lives, but they came to school, they did their homework, and they worked hard. And their parents believed in education. Made them do their homework every night. I taught these kids and they learned."

I notice the teachers on either side of Roger sliding down in their chairs. Roger clearly has a "difficult person" reputation in this group. Several others perk up, no doubt wondering how this small drama is going to unfold.

Roger continues. "Now fast forward to Massachusetts right now. Spanish kids don't care about school. Parents don't care about school. Sometimes these kids come, sometimes they don't. No big deal. They hang around the house. They watch TV, play video games. Their parents, many of them are on welfare. They don't care either. So here's the thing. I'm still teaching, but they're not learning. So what is wrong with this picture?"

With that, Roger makes a grand pleading gesture with his hands. Everybody looks at me. I decide to play it cool. I wait a beat.

"Good question, Roger. What do you think is wrong with the picture?"

"I've got some ideas, but I'm asking you. You're the consultant."

"Fair enough. Actually, I see some things in the picture that aren't wrong. You were clearly very effective with your students in Chinatown. Congratulations. I'm guessing you made a profound difference in many of their lives. What you did there worked." Here I pause.

"Sounds like you're doing the same thing here, but it isn't working."

"Got that right."

"So what are you going to do about that?"

"What do you mean, 'what am *I* going to do about that'? I'm going to teach, like I always have, but the kids don't want to learn. You can lead a horse to water." Roger pauses here for dramatic effect.

"Right. So the methods you used in Chinatown worked fabulously well. Your students learned. Sounds like those methods aren't working here. What do you do about that?"

Roger is starting to get a little bothered. "You know I'm kind of tired of hearing 'we have to fix the teachers.' Maybe it's time we fixed the kids."

"I often feel the same way, Roger. There are a lot of things about society that I don't like, that I wish were different, and I get frustrated because I don't have a lot of control over them. But I can't fix them, so I focus on what I *do* have some control over."

"Oh, come on." Roger is shifting in his seat.

"Bear with me, please, just a minute. I'm familiar with several schools in this area that have limited resources, just like yours, with students who are recent immigrants, just like yours, most from low income households, where the students are actually making good progress."

"Yeah, and it's because they have administrators who know how to keep order."

"They have effective leaders, yes. And they also have teachers who are working together, examining their teaching methods, working closely with students who are not doing well, reaching out to families. The kinds of things that you all are experimenting with right here, right now."

"Okay." Roger puts his hands up, as if in surrender. "Okay, enough, enough. I can see this is going nowhere. Thank you, Dr. Nehring, for your perspective. I asked my question. I got my answer. Thank you."

"You're welcome, Roger."

There's been a good deal of learning in the education field in recent decades about teacher efficacy and it says that teachers who believe they *can* make a difference *do* make a difference. In some quarters, though, teachers are reluctant to acknowledge a causal link between what they do instructionally and what students learn. This is because historically the profession has focused more on what a teacher does and less on what a student learns as a consequence.

As the profession has woken up to this limitation and made changes, the policy world has seized on it and reduced the relationship unfairly to test score results—simple inputs and outputs—on the basis of which teachers are rewarded or punished. Neither extreme makes sense. There are many factors at play in classroom learning, and thoughtful educators will be alert to them all. But bureaucracies and policies generally fail at subtlety.

Roger's frustration was, I guess, bound up in this dynamic. The fact that some of his students were poor and Hispanic may have provided Roger an additional excuse based on his prejudices about class and ethnicity.

THREE STEPS FORWARD

One day after a meeting, I was talking with Barbara, the vice principal who was coordinating my work with the school and who managed the teacher groups, like Gena's.

"You know, I gotta say," she said, "for the eleven years I've been an assistant principal, I've managed things like schedules, discipline codes, bathroom duty. And for the first time in my career, I am truly facilitating better teaching, you know?"

"Tell me more," I encouraged her.

"Well, some days these group leaders," she gestured to the door indicating everyone who just left, "they'll come here for a meeting, on the days when you're not here, and they'll just start talking about problems they're facing in their teaching or with their study group. And I don't mean whining—you know how teachers will vent and act like they don't *actually* want to do something about it—I don't mean that. I mean they come in here and they say 'okay, here's the problem.' Then people ask clarifying questions. Then they discuss what's really the root of this problem and ask if we're framing this problem correctly and what can the person do about it, you know?"

"That's great," I said.

"And so I serve as facilitator, you know. 'Does everybody understand the problem? Larry—let's say it's Larry who shared the problem—Is there anything else we need to know about the problem? It's like . . . my work, my job, is transformed. The teachers who are getting it don't come anymore to me as 'the administrator' to say 'what are *you* going do about it?' Instead, it's what can *we* do to navigate this thing together. And it isn't some drive-by comment in the hall, either. It's a conversation, and we follow up. We are working on it. With 'we' as a focus."

I said, "That's fantastic," and see Barbara's eyes water up.

TWO STEPS BACK

One month later, the superintendent announced his retirement. Three months after that, a new superintendent was in his place. Young, energetic, and decidedly old school, he reflected the mostly white school committee's assessment that the district's decline was due to a loss of "old values," and what was needed was a strong "traditional" leader.

With Edward Stigas, that's what they got. Edward was watchful for the first three months of his tenure—January to March. On the surface, he was approving of "the good work" being done at the high school through various initiatives, one of which was the study groups spearheaded by Barbara, for which I was consulting.

Then, one day in the middle of March, he called a meeting of all the principals and assistant principals in the district to announce "major changes." As Barbara told it, the meeting was a testosterone-charged massacre of everything fragile and promising in the district.

The new literacy approach in the three elementary schools would be closed out in June to be replaced with a textbook series chosen by the language arts supervisor, which was "more straightforward, back to basics." The middle school schedule would be "updated" to allow more electives to prepare students for "the rigors of high school and the real world." The team planning time that middle school teachers relied on to build creative programming and discuss student, would be replaced with individual teacher prep time.

At the high school, the writing center would be closed down because it was "loosey goosey." The senior research project would become optional instead of required to allow more time for remedial math courses, and the teacher study teams would be replaced with traditional department meetings focused on schedules, budgets, and discipline.

Barbara called me the next day. She told me everything that had just gone down. "Everything we've worked for is gone." She sounded numb.

I tried to console her. I said the skills and habits we'd fostered would continue, only in different form, but I knew that wasn't really true. At best, they would lie dormant waiting for the next real leader to arrive and who knew when, if ever, that would be.

CHAPTER 17: REFLECTION QUESTIONS

1. The author describes professional development approaches as "enthusiastic motivational talk" and "techniques to be implemented" and contrasts those approaches with the work featured in this chapter. How are they different?
2. A teacher might say, "I teach every day, but some of my students just don't want to learn." What responsibility does a teacher have beyond this assessment?
3. The author makes a case, through the stories in this chapter, for deep change in the teaching culture of schools. Do you agree? Explain your thinking.

SUGGESTED READING

An excellent and popular book focusing on the ways in which schools need to change in order to ensure all students learn is Richard Dufour and Robert Eaker's *Professional Learning Communities at Work*. By contrasting conventional norms with the norms of a truly excellent school, the authors make a compelling case for cultural transformation and provide practical guidance. Another fine book, by Milbrey McLaughlin and Joan Talbert, is *Building School-Based Teacher Learning Communities*. Based on decades of work with schools in the San Francisco Bay area, the authors make the case for collaborative inquiry as the defining feature of a powerful teaching culture.

EIGHTEEN

TROUBLE

By tradition and practice, there are three main parts to being a professor: research, teaching, and service. Making trouble is not officially in the job description.

Trouble doesn't always have a beginning, or if it does, finding it is like working upstream to find a river's source. I may have started thinking about mounting a protest against the test-mania that was addling our state leaders' brains when a comment Ted Sizer had made years before became so loud in my head that the only way to stop it was to act. Ted's comment was, "The silence of the universities is deafening."

This was said at a time when I was not working in a university and neither was he. But now I was back in the university setting again. I began with my pen, by writing a commentary for the periodical *Education Week*. I based the short article on a recent realization that much of the education research I found myself reading drew on test scores to warrant claims. A certain school practice may be deemed efficacious because schools that employ it see a rise in test results.

I'd pick up nearly any peer-reviewed journal in my field, leaf through it, and find frequent references to test scores to substantiate the author's claims. At the same time, the three scholarly societies that dominate the field of education had all issued public statements condemning the practice of high stakes testing.

We were, by and large, basing our work on something we condemned.

At about the time this thought rose to the surface, I was undertaking a required online training program to update my knowledge of human subjects protection for research purposes. The training program discussed historic violations of human subjects such as the injection of African-American servicemen with live syphilis virus for decades start-

175

ing in the 1930s, and grotesque Nazi experiments with death camp prisoners. No one in the world of education research, so far as I knew, was doing anything so heinous, but the same principles were in play: using results gained by unethical means, knowingly subjecting persons to potentially harmful treatments.

So I wrote my piece, calling out my colleagues on our immoral complicity, pledging to not use such test results in my own research, and inviting others to join me. I included my email address. The article was published under the headline, "First Do No Harm." From *Education Week's* fifty thousand subscribers and nearly one million web traffickers, a total of three persons contacted me to say they agreed. Interestingly, no one wrote to disagree. The silence *was* deafening.

Failure is disheartening. Spectacular failure, however, can be stimulating. It appeals to one's defiant streak. I had started writing my first book after I had failed to publish an article on a similar theme, rejected by a dozen magazines. And so, with Ted's words ringing ever louder in my ears, I began to talk up the idea of a public statement opposing high stakes testing.

First, I approached colleagues on my hall. Would they sign on? Absolutely. Encouraged, I drafted a simple statement condemning the practice and, so as not to be criticized as merely negative, I included language indicating a readiness by the undersigned to assist the state in creating an alternative assessment system.

Next, I checked around campus to make sure sending the pledge out over the university email system wouldn't get me fired. The answer: it was not political advocacy per se; it was professional activism. I decided to try to reach every education professor within the University of Massachusetts and Massachusetts State College systems. It was, after all, a simple project that I could conduct entirely from my desk.

After several weeks of emailing, an encouraging forty-one professors agreed to publicly add their names and titles to the statement. Several administrators indicated they really wanted to add their names, but worried that doing so would jeopardize their chances for various pending requests from the state. They were, nonetheless, with us in spirit.

Next came the question of how to publicize the statement. I obtained a media list from a sympathetic non-profit group based in Massachusetts and prepared a press release with a copy of the statement attached. The press release went through several drafts shared with signers of the statement and, on a day chosen for its relative absence of news, I clicked *send*.

The media responded. Several regional papers plus the Associated Press and the *Christian Science Monitor* contacted me for more information, and several stories followed the next day. Then TV called. A popular news talk show from the Boston public TV station wanted me on with the newly appointed state commissioner of education.

From my limited experience with TV, I knew I had to have my talking points ready to go and to make sure I inserted them one way or another regardless of the agenda of either the host or the other guest. This worked, and, surprisingly, the commissioner, clearly caught off guard, began back-pedaling during the interview saying the system is not perfect and can be made better.

Though it was not my intent to embarrass anyone, I was later told that I "skewered" the commissioner. This did not go unnoticed. An editorial page editor from the *Boston Globe* called shortly thereafter. We chatted. He seemed very interested in the perspective presented in the public statement. I was impressed with his thoughtful questions, but felt surprised the next day when I saw a *Globe* editorial in which the skewering came back at me.

The signers of the statement were, to the *Globe*, "ivory tower" intellectuals far removed from the realities of the classroom. And, instead of criticizing the school testing program, we should get our own education school graduates to do better on the licensure exams, the mixed results of which were cited in the editorial.

The author of the article, however, failed to mention that the licensure exam was often taken by teaching candidates who had *not* attended any of the state university or college education programs. A flurry of angry letters to the editor followed. The editor who originally contacted me called again, this time to apologize for misrepresenting the facts. No such apology, however, appeared in print.

Meanwhile, I decided, we really ought to call upon the governor, who so far had managed to float above the fray. Several well-known academics, among them Ted and Nancy, agreed to sign a letter to the governor, requesting a meeting to discuss the current testing system and possible alternatives. We got a meeting with his secretary of education. We shared our views. He listened attentively.

That was pretty much the end of it, for me. I'd run out of steam. The whole episode had been preceded by my participation in a state government committee on which I was asked to serve as part of the newly elected governor's effort to craft a vision for education for the state.

In our report to the governor, our committee made clear that high stakes tests should be done away with. The governor's "vision," which went public shortly thereafter, placed high stakes tests front and center.

NOT ON THE TEST

Sometimes I wonder why I do this work, but then, out of the blue, something really good happens.

I received an email from a man who had recently been admitted to one of our graduate programs. He said that he wanted me to know that about ten years before, he had found my book (*Why Do We Gotta Do This Stuff . . .*) in a used bookstore in LA, bought it, read it, and shortly thereafter, decided to go into teaching. It had been a big influence, he said.

Around the same time, I received another email from a former Parker School student whom I had taught from the seventh grade right through high school graduation. We'd stayed in touch while he was in college and graduate school. He'd just completed his Ph.D. and wrote to say what an important influence I had been as his teacher.

These results won't show up on any test.

CHAPTER 18: REFLECTION QUESTIONS

1. Why, in the face of overwhelming evidence to the contrary, do policy makers insist that high stakes testing is the solution for education's woes? What can you do to help the system change course?
2. Was the protest in this chapter meaningful or effective? How do people who are not policy makers influence the system for change?

SUGGESTED READING

A solid text for citizen activism is *Organizing for Social Change* by Kimberley Bobo and colleagues. It has been revised through many editions and is the bible for many grass roots progressive organizations.

VI

Big Picture

NINETEEN

BEAT GOES ON

It's 2012 and my thirtieth year in teaching. I'm reading *Education Week*, a newspaper out of our nation's capital that's part of my regular news diet. On page 1, I read about the new Common Core State Standards calling for more non-fiction reading in English Language Arts classes. I wonder what will happen to *Huckleberry Finn* as job skills increasingly drive the classroom.

I turn the page and see a big ad for the National Institute for School Leadership, the latest out-of-a-box training program for school principals, which rests on some good thinking, but ultimately is only as good as the teacher who is teaching it. I wonder how the graduate programs I teach in will survive against big, sexy offerings like this.

In the "News in Brief" section, I see a small piece about Tennessee making teacher ratings public. It stirs my anger over our national testing and ranking manias, and the bad practice it spawns, and the corruption it seeds.

Turn the page. I see an ad that shouts "Attention Results-oriented School Leaders!" promoting a "research-proven" reading program. I cringe at "results" and the politically driven demand for it and the growing business orientation of schools around the measurement of return-on-investment.

Turn the page. Another ad: "PLC at Work," an announcement of upcoming "institutes." I know this topic well. PLC stands for Professional Learning Community—a culture of collaborative inquiry to which a school aspires. But in the world of education, PLC has become the latest buzzword, the latest formula for success, and in many schools, just a new word for the same old bad meetings. Let's do our PLC today.

On the next page, I spot an article about Twitter as a teaching tool with elementary students tweeting their parents, and I think, okay, imaginative use of technology. The article goes on to report how teachers around the country are quietly inventing interesting uses for social media. I feel a little surge of hope.

I turn the page. I see a big photo of a very confident-looking hipster addressing a room of conservatively dressed teachers in go-to-convention mode with conference lanyards. The hipster sports a t-shirt, long hair, and a goatee. He is in mid-strut at the front of the room, his arms up in a big gesture, like Moses. The article is all about Google and its "strategic push into the education market." More smart non-educators telling us how we're missing the boat, and how we need to get on board.

The next page announces "Community Schools" in the headline. It's the continuation of a page 1 story. There are photos of kids twirling on a playground, bending over a Lego robot, leaning over a chessboard. I go back to page 1. I read about a burgeoning movement that builds local schools as hubs for community services, supported by new federal money. I feel a little tingle of optimism.

SCHOOL AS CONTESTED SPACE

I'm re-reading Herbert Kliebard's *Struggle for the American Curriculum 1893–1958*, which I'll be teaching for the foundational course that all our beginning doctoral students take. It is apparent from Kliebard's historical account that school in the United States has been a contested space. It is where interest groups representing varied and shifting convictions jockey for the lead.

Now the developmentalists are in control. Now the traditionalists. Now the social efficiency advocates. Now the social justice advocates. They represent widely diverse opinions on the ends and means of schooling.

Some say schooling should fire the imagination of the child. Others say schooling should build the child's cultural literacy. Some say schooling should meet the economic needs of society. Others say schooling should erase patterns of privilege and marginalization based on race, wealth, and gender. When there is war, a down economy, or other threats to our national identity, the traditionalists and social efficiency advocates rise. At other times, developmentalists and social justice advocates find an opening and wedge their way in.

All these groups make themselves known through reports commissioned by governors and college presidents, speeches to prominent organizations, policies enacted by state agencies, teacher associations that advance a new instructional approach, social movements that find expression in civic organizations.

Meanwhile, teacher unions squabble with administrators. Coalitions are formed, new curricula get written, parties are organized, ideologies codified, fads advanced, textbooks revised, laws passed. Each school board member brings his own agenda. Every teacher and administrator has a different angle. And all the players are regularly replaced. All of this is happening all the time across the vast, chaotic landscape of American schooling, with no singular direction taken by the whole at any given moment.

In some respects, this is not news. It conjures an image of vibrant democracy a la Walt Whitman or Alexis de Tocqueville. It is the healthy, continuous working-out of who we are as a nation. But here's the thing: in my day job, I read a great deal about the traits of high performing schools and there is a large body of research finding that collective attributes are what makes the difference in education.

Excellent schools have a *shared* vision and mission. The teachers *collaboratively* examine their practice and build a *shared* language for instruction. Teachers assume *shared* responsibility for student learning and possess a strong sense of *collective* efficacy. In short, a good school has a clear sense of purpose and everyone is on board with it. It would appear that the perpetually contested state of our schools is at odds with excellence.

When the Lab School was being conceived, I said to myself and anyone who was interested, "If people feel a part of something, they care; and when they care, they work hard." When the Parker School was young and fragile, I reassured myself and others by saying that "At least everyone is rowing in the same direction."

When I served as chair of the board of trustees for a brand new charter school, I printed the school's mission statement at the top of every board agenda and referred to it during meetings as the basis for all our deliberations. Within the Coalition of Essential Schools, the organization with which all of these schools has been connected, a set of shared ideas called "The Ten Common Principles" steers the work.

In many, perhaps most, mainstream public high schools where I have worked or visited, teachers view their classrooms as a personal domain, the door of which can shut out the disruptive clamor of the outside world. All that clamor may be the working-out-of- who-we-are-as-a-nation, but children need consistency and all those teachers who do their best to ignore or subvert all those outside forces know it.

So we are left with a conundrum: the essence of democracy is contested space, and the essence of a good school is shared vision. It may be that mission-driven schools situated within the public sector offer a solution. A charter school in Massachusetts, for example, is accountable to the state. Every five years, it must prove itself financially, organizationally, and educationally viable, or it will be shut down. It is led by a self-renewing board of trustees, chosen, in part, for their assent to the school's mission. Teachers are hired on the basis of their assent to the mission and families choose the school because of its mission. Collective attributes are well in evidence in most charter schools whether they are the kind with uniforms and single file in the halls, or the kind with everybody on a first name basis.

Charter schools aren't the only variety of mission-driven schools. Some districts have pilot schools and theme-based schools. The Lab School was a home-grown school-within-a-school, a kind of charter school before there were charters. What they share is choice and a mission. The hazard is the balkanizing influence such schools may have on society at large, and a tendency to attract families that are especially interested in education. While that may be most families, it leaves behind children who are in the greatest need and who stand to benefit the most from an excellent school.

DO THE MATH

It's Labor Day, and we are hosting dinner with friends whose children are roughly the same age as our own and whom we got to know many years before through school. Kate, who has recently launched a teaching career after seeing her two sons safely into their teens, is talking about the first two days of school the previous week with her seventh graders. Kate teaches English.

"This year I have 140 students," she says.

"That's in five classes?" I ask, expecting yes.

"No. Six."

"Whoa. I didn't think that was still even legal."

"There are seven periods in a day. I teach six, I get one prep, and I get lunch—every other day—because I have lunch duty."

"I remember my first year teaching," I say, "at Middle Valley Middle School. I had three sections of social studies, two sections of English, and one business class."

As I say this, I feel it's a mistake. It makes school teaching sound like something I grew out of, the implication being Kate has not. But I silently do the math on 140 students, an exercise I've done countless times. I don't say it out loud because I don't want to discourage Kate, and because she already knows it all too well.

If a teacher assigns a writing exercise once a week, and reads each student's paper, spending ten minutes on it, she generates 1,400 minutes of work. That's just over twenty-three hours. If the school day runs seven hours, and she needs an additional hour each day for planning and other managerial tasks (beyond her prep period, which often gets chewed up with small things), she's up to a workweek of sixty-three hours. That's an eleven hour day, five days a week, plus eight hours on the weekend. And still, she's giving each student only ten minutes of individual attention.

The conversation has moved on to a recap of summer adventures: camping, kayaking, and a day hike up Mt Monadnock. But I'm stuck on

Kate's casual revelation, and I'm going back in my mind to Ted Sizer's imperative (get the numbers down) and how most schools have a student to teacher ratio of about thirteen to one if you add up all the professionally credentialed adults in the building and divide it into the total number of students.

Once in a while, you come across a school that has figured out how to take advantage of that favorable ratio—such as the Parker School—and how it means, not a mammoth input of new resources, but a radical rethinking of roles and curriculum, and how most schools and most communities are unable to think their way past the current system.

I wish it were as simple as "we need more money." It's not. It's about subverting the dominant culture and about changing the way we do school, which is a much, much more difficult task.

CHAPTER 19: REFLECTION QUESTIONS

1. How does the tension between school as a contested space and the drive for excellence play out in your experience?
2. Is there a way to have excellent schools while respecting the contested nature of democracy?
3. How can we take better advantage of the favorable student to teacher ratio in most schools? What stands in our way? How do we overcome the barriers?

SUGGESTED READING

In *Doing School: How We Are Creating a Generation of Stressed-out, Materialistic, Mis-educated Students*, author Denise Clark Pope chronicles the daily lives of five students in a California High School and finds what the title declares. It is an eloquent diagnosis of our fundamental educational problems.

TWENTY

CORNER BAR

I'm having lunch with Rachel, a colleague ten years older than me. She's been an academic her whole career. It's a warm, sunny day in August, the week before classes start. We are seated at an outdoor café table at the Starbucks on campus.

Rachel says, "So what are you going to do now that you have tenure?"

I say, "For six years, I've been running on a hamster wheel with a poker behind me. Poker's gone, and I'm still running. They've got me well trained."

Rachel says, without missing a beat, "You shouldn't think that way. Really. You've got this amazing opportunity that almost no one in our society gets. You've got huge job security. You've got enormous freedom." She pauses, like she's thinking how to really make her point. "You've got to think big. What do you want to accomplish in the next ten years? What are you passionate about?"

Rachel's remark stays with me for several weeks as the semester gets underway. Start another school? Build a school reform organization? Those have been, at times in my life, the very thing I was hungry to do. But I'm not feeling it.

Take the starting a school idea. I know intimately some of the ways that can go. In the end, if it goes well, you get a school. And you can get a very good one that really and truly has an impact on many lives. This is a very worthy aspiration. One I could fail at just as well as I might succeed. But it's not feeling mysterious or unknown, or enticing.

Okay, what about building a school reform organization? I haven't led one, but I've stood close by someone who has. I watched it rise and took part in its work. I watched it nip at the margins of the mainstream, become part of a national conversation. Then I watched the mainstream flow on. I watched the annual conference get smaller and witnessed the struggle for funding.

A thriving organization will not go on forever. It will have its day. I've spent decades watching schools and school reform organizations, working inside them, reading about them, and writing about them. They come and go. It is in the nature of everything to come and go. What matters?

I have been a principal, a writer, a consultant to school districts, an activist, a researcher, a troublemaker. Mostly I've been a teacher. How much difference have I made playing any one of these roles?

I think about people I know who have had an obviously large impact in the field, such as Ted Sizer. But even Ted's impact is finite. The Coalition of Essential Schools will not last forever. And Ted, I am sure, had days when he felt like a failure.

Just do good work, I tell myself. Whatever role I play, just do good work.

I attended a writers' conference at Wesleyan University in 1988. A hundred aspiring writers gathered for a week to learn from a handful of established writers. There were some big names, prizewinners, people who were known out in the world of newspapers and magazines and talk shows and office conversation.

One, however, was a highly competent but not-so-famous sports writer. He led a session I attended. He said some writers are great maestros playing in great concert halls. But he was content, he said, to be the guy who plays piano in the corner bar.

ENDLESS FIELDS OF CORN

One morning, after riding my bicycle for hours through endless fields of corn, I came to a town. This was on a bicycle ride across America in 2011. My route took me through the town's one little neighborhood of square houses on square lots. In front of one house, a man mowed his small yard. It seemed pathetic. Millions of acres of corn, a little dot of a town, and, in the middle of the dot, a guy riding his lawn mower in a tiny circle.

Maybe, in the grand scheme of everything, that's all any of us really does. In the few seconds I observed him, I noticed he was doing a careful job. And then, I was out the other side of the town, which ended as abruptly as it began, and I was rolling through endless fields of corn.

What really matters in life is when it's your turn, you carry the torch. Then somebody else takes it up. You all work to keep the flame alive. The goal is not to be famous, live forever, or be remembered long after you're gone. The goal is do good work—a useful mantra.

Garrison Keillor invokes it as part of a tag for his daily radio show about poetry. Before he signs off, he says, "Do good work."

Once, long ago, I drew satisfaction from digging a ditch because I took care to do it well. When I started out as a teacher at Middle Valley, I struggled to learn what good teaching is and felt satisfaction when I started to sort it out—just do good work. In leading startup schools, the greatest reward came from the many small signals in the course of the day that we were making a positive incremental difference in the lives of our students. And in my teaching and research at the university it's come from a class that goes well, a research study that stands up to the reviewers. It's all about doing good work.

BALANCE?

In my early post-tenure phase, I was striving for balance. I was sporting a mindset that said *work hard, but don't let work be the only thing in your life.*

I got more involved in our church, I took more time on household chores, and I took Saturdays off, except for a couple hours of work in the morning. If my self-imposed, ambitious deadline for something appeared to require too much attention, I moved the deadline back enough to feel relaxed about it.

There've been other times when I felt this way—balanced. There was the period after we moved into our first house, before we had children, when I rode my bike to school on good-weather days and returned home feeling like Mr. Rogers. There was a period after I stepped down from being principal and returned to the classroom full time. I relished early mornings, when I stood in front of our school with a steaming cup of coffee, not bothered by half-a-dozen urgent, emotionally charged, unresolved issues. I watched the students arrive and felt reasonably assured that the plan I had for my day with them would be what actually happened.

But each time I achieved balance, it didn't last. Maybe I was secretly bored. Maybe balance is boring.

One day during this early post-tenure phase, my dean sent out an email to the faculty asking if anyone was interested in collaborating with universities in Israel and Ireland. That could mean a lot of different things, none of which I asked about. I just wrote back, impulsively, "I'm game."

It turned out our university's new chancellor, dreamy-eyed with a vision of global reach, was signing partnership agreements seemingly with every university president around the world who was willing. Faculty were being encouraged to "collaborate." I often tell school leaders who hire me as a consultant, "Don't collaborate for the sake of collaborating. Do it in service of a meaningful goal."

I was thinking about this when, a few months later, I found myself sitting at a conference table with two professors from Israel, two from

Northern Ireland, and a colleague from UMass Lowell. We'd all answered the call to "collaborate" and had been brought together for three
days in June, given a conference room with snacks and told, "figure
something out."

Talking around our conference table, we realized there is an increasing mismatch between what schools teach and test, on the one hand, and
what society needs, on the other. That is, many schools around the world
have to teach to a state test that requires memorization and simple ana-
lytical skills. Testing mania has gone global.

At the same time, civic life and many jobs require creative problem
solving, collaboration, intellectual openness and other complex traits that
don't show up on a test. Most schools teach to the test because that's what
counts. This is especially true in poor communities where scores are low
and test pressure is intense. Which means kids who need high quality
schooling the most get the worst test prep drivel. We wondered if there
might be outlier schools in poor communities that knock the socks off the
test, but also teach all those other, more important skills. The world could
learn from them.

We wrote up our idea in formal apply-for-research-grant language
and began to shop it around. We submitted it to half a dozen funders and
got turned down everywhere. One day, my dean said, "Have you considered applying for a Fulbright?"

I hadn't, but I did, and to my amazement, I got a grant, the William J.
Fulbright Program of the United States Department of State, to study
outlier schools in Northern Ireland. We also received a small grant to
fund the U.S. portion of our study. We could, at least, proceed with the
U.S. and UK. I would soon be off to Northern Ireland for five months.

Before I got the Fulbright, the story I'd invented for my work life
ended with me getting tenure. It was hard to imagine something beyond
tenure because: A) all my energy was focused on it and B) not getting it
felt like an end, too—the alternate, undesirable end. Which is why earn-
ing tenure left me a bit lost. I cleaned the house. I kept spinning on my
hamster wheel.

Now, all of a sudden, there was material for a new narrative. It was an
exciting narrative, one in which my work life is a story of expanding
circles of interest. At Middle Valley Middle School my interest was in
changing up my classroom practice. With the Lab School it was about
changing the practice of several classrooms at once. At the Parker School
it was about re-imagining the structure and purpose of an entire school.
At the university it was about influencing the field across a region and,
through research, on an even broader scale.

With the Fulbright and the international study it supported, the work
moved to an international arena. This was starting to feel like a tale of
global domination. I reigned myself in. Okay, it *was* a narrative with

direction and meaning. I was off the hamster wheel. The clutter piles started to re-appear back home, and I didn't do anything about it.

CHAPTER 20: REFLECTION QUESTIONS

1. What really matters in a career?
2. What is your greatest point of leverage for social change?
3. How do you make a difference?
4. Is "do good work" a sufficient mantra? Why or why not?
5. Is it possible to be passionate about your work and live a balanced life?
6. Should a career have an arc, a kind of logical and satisfying trajectory? Are such narratives that we create for ourselves imagined or do they reflect the facts?

SUGGESTED READING

Michael Carroll's *Awake at Work: 35 Practical Buddhist Principles for Discovering Clarity and Balance in the Midst of Work's Chaos* offers thoughtful guidance that goes much deeper than most career happiness books. *Making a Living While Making a Difference* by Melissa Everett offers practical advice for joining your deep passions with your vocation.

TWENTY-ONE

LADDER UP A WALL

"You'll be doing archival research as a major part of this class," I said and watched the impact register on my students' faces. Their faces appeared somewhere between worried and curious.

It was the first meeting of the doctoral foundations course. I wanted to try something I thought was exciting, but I was afraid my students would see it as deadly boring or scary. I wanted my students to have the experience of seeing over the high walls erected by the educational fads that make up our daily existence and realize they are neither permanent nor necessary. They are made by people and they can be unmade.

One day, back when I was starting work on my dissertation, I drove to Quincy, Massachusetts, to visit the Thomas Crane Public Library. Quincy is where Francis Parker, first superintendent of the Quincy schools, served from 1875 to 1880. My plan was to explore the library and see what items it might have dating to that period.

I was hoping I could find town annual reports, including the annual school committee report, and, if I was lucky, a local newspaper from the era. I was lucky. The annual town reports were lined up neatly in bound volumes on a bookcase dating back deep into the 1800s. Also, there was a newspaper, *The Quincy Patriot*, which was available on microfilm. The newspaper was in continuous publication all through Francis Parker's superintendency. Not only that, the microfilm reader photocopied any page I wanted for a dime a sheet. I dug in.

As I sat at the massive reading table, carefully turning the pages of the report from the year 1874, I was struck that the events described, though well over 100 years old, were also being currently considered:

> The persistent injunctions of the Committee . . . have had a manifest
> influence in diminishing the dependence of both pupil and teacher

upon the textbook. But it is still too great. (Quincy Annual Report, 1874,
   p. 6)

Though the language is old-fashioned, the issue is as fresh as the latest conversation of parents gathering at the school bus stop down the road from my house. How interesting that: A) they had textbooks back then, and B) some people were concerned that teachers and students relied upon them too much.

I got up, went back to the shelf and pulled off the Annual Report from 1876, the year after Francis Parker arrived. Sure enough, a "Superintendent's Report" appears part way through. Reading it, I learn of a "truancy" problem. Truancy is a quaint term, but school attendance is an important benchmark of success. What really got my attention, as I turned the page, was Parker's solution to the truancy problem:

   The shortening of the school year, and its division into three terms,
   with vacations at the close of each, has, I think, remedied the difficul-
   ty. . . . (Quincy Annual Report, 1876, p. 120).

Parker's solution to truancy was to *shorten* the school year and add more vacations. The kids were sick and tired of school and needed a break. In the volume from another year, I read that Parker was concerned about state exams intruding on school life. In another, he wrote about his efforts to keep spending per pupil down in order to not overtax the community.

I was getting a distinct impression that many of the issues we face today are nothing new. This felt liberating. We are not alone, I thought. How odd to be made to feel not alone by a document nearly a hundred-fifty years old about people who are all long dead.

And as others have faced these issues, my thought continued, they have attempted solutions from which we may learn: What worked for them? What didn't work for them? How did partisans behave? What were the short-term results? What were the long-term results? How did the players interact with one another?

Though our own stories are yet unfolding, these stories from so many years ago have fully run their course. We can, in a way, see our possible futures in these yellowed and fragile pages.

This is what I wanted my doctoral students to experience. Which is why, two class sessions later, when students brought the results of their initial search for local historical sources to class, I was eager to hear not just what they found, but what they felt before, during, and after their search.

"I found this amazing collection of personal papers from my school district's first superintendent from 1909 until 1917. Apparently, his family donated the papers in the 1960s and somebody at the library organized them a bit, but as far as I know, no one has ever really done anything with them."

This was Tanya, who teaches high school science. She continued, "It's amazing. I started reading some of them. They're all in labeled boxes, like twenty boxes of reports and letters and stuff. Apparently, at one point there was some issue about cheating on a school exam and a whole bunch of students who were involved. I've only just started reading. It's utterly fascinating."

Rhonda, a curriculum specialist at another district spoke up. "I went to the local history room at our library just to see what was there, and I found all the annual reports for the town going back to the 1840s. It's amazing. They're all just right there and you can pull them off the shelf. I was reading from the 1880s about a new teaching technique that all the teachers were learning from this professor who was at the normal school nearby. It was more activity-based and less 'passive.'" Rhonda makes air quotes. "I mean . . . *progressives* . . . in the 1880s? It was like it could have happened last week."

Todd, a middle school Spanish teacher reported his findings. "They have a section in the school library with like old memorabilia, and, apparently, there was a literary magazine that was published all through the 1940s and 1950s called *The Lyceum*. They have every issue for something like eighteen years, and they've got boxes of related papers: printing bills, rejected manuscripts."

With each story, I felt the positive energy in the room increase.

At what level in education should we expose the fact that social institutions are invented, that the way we do things is just made up by people responding to circumstances? Place all people between the ages of thirteen and seventeen in a red brick building between the hours of 8 a.m. and 3 p.m. for 180 days each year. We made that up. Require the young people to sit still for periods of forty-five minutes with a three-minute exercise break every hour. We made that up. Insist that they become proficient with simple mental tasks and memorize stories while sitting there for four years. We made that up, too.

If we teach it nowhere else, then at least at the doctoral level, we have to make sure that our students learn not only the contingent nature of our social institutions, but understand how they came to be and begin to imagine what it will take to change them.

READY ENOUGH

I used to think I should be completely ready when I enter a classroom, but now my aspiration is to be *ready enough*. Truth is, I never *was* completely ready, even back when I thought I was supposed to be.

It's September of 1982, my first year teaching. I teach ninth grade English for three of my six classes. Grammar is the topic today. I can't remember why, since I don't think there was a district-wide curriculum. I can't remember ever sitting with the other teachers to find out what everybody else taught—as unbelievable as that may sound.

There was a big, fat, gray anthology of stories, essays, and poems. There was also a small, fat, orange book of grammar. To an extent, there was an agreed upon ninth grade English curriculum: it was these two books. There was also a state syllabus. I was not given a copy, so I requested one from the State department of education. I was pretty excited when it arrived because I was hoping it would lead me through the year. I imagined when Bonnie, the other ninth grade English teacher, or Hank, the eighth grade English teacher asked what I was teaching and why, I could say smugly, "we're doing so and so right now as part of the composition strand in the state syllabus."

For whatever reason—little orange book, big state syllabus, something Bonnie or Hank said—I was going to teach the parts of speech today. The state syllabus included sample activities, which I occasionally read for inspiration. One activity involved preparing cards with example words for the different parts of speech, scrambling them up, then inviting the class to sort them.

I pulled a chunk of index cards and a marker from the drawer in my desk where random supplies resided. The state syllabus even suggested words, which I copied, adding a few of my own. Cool, I thought, as I wrote a word on each card in large letters, using my best penmanship. I imagined my students intrigued by this giant word puzzle. I reveled in the exploratory nature of the lesson. Grammar could be fun. It did not have to be all drill. Students could naturally perceive the parts of speech in the patterns of everyday words.

I started the lesson by shuffling all the cards at my desk, telling everyone that today we would be playing cards.

"Can you do that?" asked Jessica, always thinking about what's permitted.

I thought about saying, "Today, we'll just break the rules a little," but thought better of it, given the rule breaking tendencies of some of Jessica's classmates, including Todd Harper.

I put the word cards up on the bulletin board, and everyone jerked and scraped their desks over to the right side of the room.

"So, if you had to group these words according to words that are similar in the way you might use them in a sentence, how would you group them?"

"I'd put word and bird together because they rhyme," said Rhonda Rodenton.

I wasn't sure how to handle that, so I just put them together. I pulled the pin off *bird*, moved *bird* over to *word*, and stuck the pin back in.

"Put house over there, too," Reggie called out.

"That doesn't rhyme!" Rhonda said.

"They're all nouns," said Reggie.

"Add tree," someone else called out.

"And lamp."

"And cat."

"Oh, I got another set!" cried Martin. "You've got under, between, and over."

Pretty quickly, all the words were correctly sorted, and we had correctly labeled each group with the parts of speech. No sooner did I feel a surge of pedagogical triumph than a sinking feeling struck: What next?

Somehow, I had imagined this taking a half hour, and then we would follow it with the continuing discussion of the short story we were reading for the remainder of the period. I looked at the clock. Class began at 10:36 a.m. and ran to 11:19. It was now 10:40.

I panicked. "Okay. Good job, everybody. Please scoot your desks back and take out "The Scarlet Ibis.""

There were several problems with my lesson, the biggest of which was how long I spent preparing it. Between the having of an idea, reviewing the state syllabus, locating the index cards, identifying forty words, and filling out the cards, I'd spent close to an hour on the lesson's first section. One hour of prep for four minutes of teaching—a fifteen to one ratio. At that rate, teaching 20 hours per week, I could anticipate 300 hours of prep time.

That wasn't the only problem. There was also no clear purpose. Why did we group words? What exactly did I expect my students to *learn* from this exercise? And because there was no purpose, there was no follow-up.

Had my purpose been for students to be able to identify and name parts of speech, I might have had them. . . .

- break into small groups and make their own card sets, which I would check and then hand to another team to sort
- turn to our big orange grammar book and introduce the section on parts of speech
- break into eight teams, one for each part of speech, and have each team assemble a list of words
- each become a part of speech and walk around the room spouting, identifying which part of speech each student in class was playing
- sample sentences and ask them to identify words in the sentence according to their parts of speech
- all go on a field trip consisting of one lap around the first floor of the building looking for parts of speech inspired by what they see and hear
- complete Mad Libs, filling in the right parts of speech in the blank spaces
- create Mad Libs for each other
- create nonsense sentences that were grammatically correct from lists of parts of speech

- play parts-of-speech Jeopardy
- look at favorite sayings and identify favorite words according to their parts of speech

But I didn't. The main reason I didn't in the moment that my clever, way-too-short activity ended is that I didn't know how. I hadn't been teaching for thirty-plus years, and I didn't have a repertoire—one of the benefits of experience.

Now, if something isn't going the way I want it to, or if I have a better idea in the moment, I have enough stored up ideas and enough confidence to change it up, to experiment.

ANXIETY DREAM

When I was a new teacher, I used to panic as the time to class got shorter and no lesson idea was forthcoming. I'd panic, also, if the idea required a huge amount of effort—days searching for readings or hours making props for a four-minute activity. Now, as the clock ticks down to class, I know I will have a plan when the time comes. I always do. And I always do because I have years of ideas rattling around in my head. And when I really need to pull something together, I can.

I used to have anxiety dreams about teaching. For example, in one dream it's summertime, and I am completely relaxed, sitting by my in-law's pool three hundred miles from home. I suddenly realize it's the first day of school and I'm missing it.

I quickly gather my family and all our things and hop in the car. We're driving home, the kids are in the back seat totally confused about why we just left in the middle of summer vacation, and I'm thinking how I haven't planned the new course I'm supposed to teach and how I was going to do that next week, but I can't because school has started and I'm not there.

Suddenly, in the way that dreams will shift, I'm in my classroom. It's the third day of school and my students are asking me where I was for the first two days. They tell me they were doing fine without me. They've been playing cards and hanging out. They say nobody stopped by or seemed to notice I was absent.

Todd and Rhonda are in one corner of the room throwing dice against the wall. I try to get everyone's attention, but they act like I'm not there. I try to speak, but no words come out. They are all very self-sufficiently engaged in activities I have nothing to do with.

I don't have these types of dreams anymore. In fact, I had a recent dream where I suddenly realize I have a three-hour graduate class to plan. I check my watch and it is starting in five minutes. I think fast, and several ideas pop up. I arrange them in my mind while I'm walking to class.

I teach the class and the plan works. The students have no idea that the class got planned only minutes before. Students are fully engaged. I'm strutting around giving instructions that everyone eagerly follows. There's laughter and excitement. And there's this little voice, like a dream narrator, and the little voice is saying, *this dream is not realistic.* It is saying, *you're making this all up just to make yourself feel good.*

An argument ensues between the part of my mind that created this lovely dream and the part that doubts it. The creative part says, *I know how to plan lessons fast and I have lots of experience.* The doubting part says, *don't fool yourself. It isn't that easy. Don't get cocky.*

That's when I wake up. It's the end of August, a week before classes start for the fall semester. Most of my planning is done. I get up, go to my desk, and start to detail the first few sessions. I know what I want to do, but I write it out: the objectives, the agenda, the plan, the assignment. I've taught long enough to know that much of the plan will shift after I meet my students, so I don't fuss over the details.

I do this each morning for an hour until the semester begins. And on the first day, I still don't feel completely ready, but I've learned that being completely ready is the wrong way to be because my students will alter the plan. So, instead, I tell myself that I'm ready enough. I'm ready to begin.

CHAPTER 21: REFLECTION QUESTIONS

1. When planning a lesson, how ready is *ready enough*? How do you know when to stop?
2. Is it possible, as an experienced teacher, to become cavalier in planning lessons? How do you find the right balance between faith in your teaching ability and a high standard for instruction?

SUGGESTED READING

For a fascinating book in which twenty prominent school reformers reflect on how their views have changed over the years, read *I Used to Think . . . and Now I Think . . .: Twenty Leading Educators Reflect on the Work of School Reform* compiled by Richard F. Elmore.